The Electric Guitar Handbook

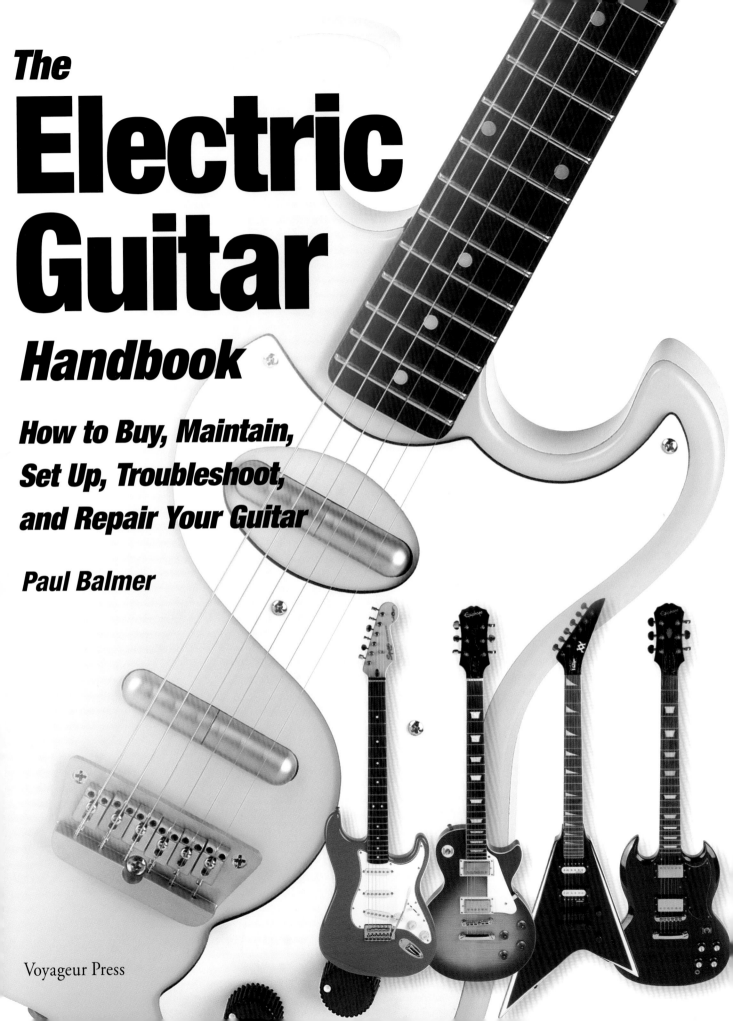

The Electric Guitar Handbook

How to Buy, Maintain, Set Up, Troubleshoot, and Repair Your Guitar

Paul Balmer

Voyageur Press

Contents

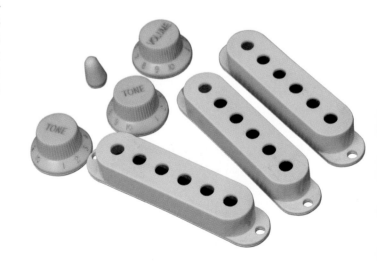

Introduction

My first guitar was impossible to play, so I gave up and swapped it for a snare drum!

Luckily a schoolteacher saw the guitar and explained that it just needed the right strings and a set-up. As supplied, it was a half-size Spanish guitar, set up 'Hawaiian' with steel strings, and impossible to fret. So I swapped the drum back and have had a great time with my guitars for the last 50 years. It was this 'near miss' experience that compelled me to write the Haynes 'Guitar Manuals' – and especially this one.

I believe your first electric guitar is the most important guitar you'll ever own. If it's tuneable and the strings are fret-able without recourse to blood and too many blisters, then you can start learning; if *not*, then you may also give up. Make no mistake – you'll need perseverance and patience with the music side of learning, but *five minutes a day and you will learn to play*!

However, you desperately need your guitar to be in tune, fun, and sounding good, just to get you over the first hurdles.

This book should help you choose the guitar that makes the sound that drove you to want to learn in the first place – be that 'Death Metal' or 'Rockabilly', retro pop or Chicago blues, 'three chords and the truth' or a new genre entirely that you are about to invent.

Once you have the right guitar, this book will help you set it up so that it plays like a dream and inspires you to keep going.

In the 21st century that guitar need not be expensive. Later on I 'case-study' a series of guitars that are mostly very affordable but cover a lot of genres in terms of their sound. Modern-day economics mean that most of these guitars arrive at the point of sale unfinished – finishing or 'set-up' is labour-intensive, and therefore expensive – but this sad 'bean-counters' charter' is easily remedied.

Pay attention to 'sound'. You'll progress quicker if your guitar makes the sound you strive for in your head; so good-sounding amps and effects can help, especially in the early stages.

Get that 'Brit pop' sound on a budget.

> 'A good guitar is one that makes you want to play – you look at the clock and an hour has passed in a moment.'

The cheaper guitars are the ones that will most likely need some work, but it's all doable if you have basic DIY skills and are patient and methodical. Most serious errors are recoverable, so try your best, and if you have difficulty consult a luthier or a guitar tech – your local music store will know one.

You may need a few specialist tools: these will make working on your guitar a pleasure and will avoid you damaging it. The Internet revolution means they're all just a Jiffy bag away!

You will need some courage, as guitars seem a little fragile and the correct adjustment is often a matter of a few thousandths of an inch! However, the guitar is a very personal instrument and you'll become the world expert on your style of playing – and your perfect set-up is something that only you are truly qualified to judge.

So be confident – experiment, get it wrong a few times and then get it right! All the world's great luthiers have made mistakes. The trick is to learn from them and then do it better each time.

Everything in this manual is equally applicable to your eventual 'custom shop special' – because even that may not be set up entirely the way you like it!

So remember 'it's just a plank of wood' – then try and find the special synergy called *magic*!

Paul Balmer
March 2011

This simple set-up works a treat! '5 watts of awesome power!'

Anatomy of an electric guitar

Where it really all began – Leo and Lester's great idea. This 'exploded' Tele demonstrates that all the essential elements have changed little in over half a century.

Electric guitars vary in detail, but much of what matters first emerged in 1950 with Leo Fender's Esquire, followed in 1952 by Gibson's Les Paul: two great pickups, a solid plank of wood and an accurately fretted neck. Put these ingredients together in the right order and you have a versatile machine that will see you through almost any gig.

Strap button

'Ashtray'

Neck body join Gibson and Epiphone tend towards traditional tenon joints, while Fender and many others avoid complicated luthiery, and when the neck wears out simply bolt on a new one! Expensive guitars may have a 'through neck', which is integral to the body. A bolt-on neck is a lot easier to fix.

Body Made of a good hardwood, though not necessarily the traditional 'tone woods'. Leo Fender even prototyped in pine, and that worked! Gibson use mahogany and maple, others use ash, alder, rosewood, basswood and a number of exotic hybrids – the shape is about ergonomics and comfort on the hip, so almost anything goes. Semi-solids can be lighter and 'woodier'. Even plywood has its fans!

Bridge pickup The heart of the twang – alnico pickups sound more convincing than ceramics in many applications. Generally single coils enhance more high frequencies. Humbuckers 'buck the hum' and can sound darker due to a mid-frequency bias.

An adjustable bridge Pitch and intonation is more critical on the electric guitar than the acoustic guitar, as amplification shows up the tiniest error. Most modern electric guitars have micro-adjustable saddles. Height adjustment makes for more comfortable playing. 'Thru body' stringing is a sustain-enhancing bonus, originally tried and tested on the Fender Champion steel guitar.

Jack socket The output to your amplifier – simple, electronically 'unbalanced', but mostly effective.

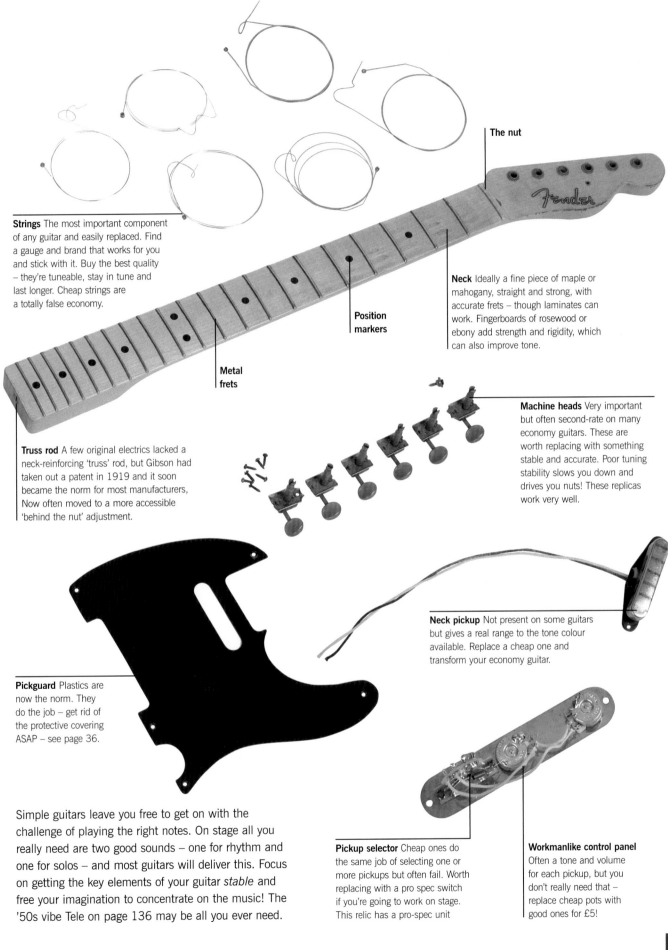

Strings The most important component of any guitar and easily replaced. Find a gauge and brand that works for you and stick with it. Buy the best quality – they're tuneable, stay in tune and last longer. Cheap strings are a totally false economy.

The nut

Neck Ideally a fine piece of maple or mahogany, straight and strong, with accurate frets – though laminates can work. Fingerboards of rosewood or ebony add strength and rigidity, which can also improve tone.

Position markers

Metal frets

Truss rod A few original electrics lacked a neck-reinforcing 'truss' rod, but Gibson had taken out a patent in 1919 and it soon became the norm for most manufacturers, Now often moved to a more accessible 'behind the nut' adjustment.

Machine heads Very important but often second-rate on many economy guitars. These are worth replacing with something stable and accurate. Poor tuning stability slows you down and drives you nuts! These replicas work very well.

Neck pickup Not present on some guitars but gives a real range to the tone colour available. Replace a cheap one and transform your economy guitar.

Pickguard Plastics are now the norm. They do the job – get rid of the protective covering ASAP – see page 36.

Simple guitars leave you free to get on with the challenge of playing the right notes. On stage all you really need are two good sounds – one for rhythm and one for solos – and most guitars will deliver this. Focus on getting the key elements of your guitar *stable* and free your imagination to concentrate on the music! The '50s vibe Tele on page 136 may be all you ever need.

Pickup selector Cheap ones do the same job of selecting one or more pickups but often fail. Worth replacing with a pro spec switch if you're going to work on stage. This relic has a pro-spec unit

Workmanlike control panel Often a tone and volume for each pickup, but you don't really need that – replace cheap pots with good ones for £5!

ELECTRIC GUITAR MANUAL

Buying an electric guitar

This is a great time to buy an electric guitar. Bargains abound from most of the classic marques: Fender, Gibson, Gretsch and Rickenbacker are available in affordable 'versions' branded as Squier, Epiphone, Ibanez, 'Vintage' and a dozen others. This is also a good time to strike out and perhaps purchase a radically different type of guitar that once seemed out of reach – retro, rockabilly, semi-acoustic, flying V etc. These new options are usually made to a discount price in the Far East. Though as delivered they're rarely 'ready to play', all the ingredients are there ready for refinement and fine-tuning. A good set-up and perhaps later some boutique pickups and you could well have a professional instrument for less than £500.

LEFT An Epiphone DOT.

RIGHT A Squier Strat.

New electric guitars have never been better. Most of the classic designs were invented over 60 years ago, but the hit-and-miss nature of early construction has been replaced by CNC (computer numerical control), which ensures a consistency of tolerance in their largely component-assembled construction. This may all sound a little cold, but by and large it works in our favour – the ideal shapes and tolerances have been established through craft and experience – the new technology merely ensures that those ideal dimensions are achieved consistently.

That said, the micro-detail required in getting a musical instrument to play in tune, comfortably and with the right set-up for your style is a different matter – hence this book.

Many advanced players stick to the classic winning formulas with their guitars – Eric Clapton plays a guitar not unlike a '50s Fender Strat ('S' type), and Slash plays a '50s-style Gibson Les Paul ('LP' type): these guitars deliver. First-time buyers can buy CNC versions of these shapes assembled in China but fully licensed from their original sources, and that licensing ensures a degree of confidence for the buyer – the original manufacturers have their name on the line. Many other unlicensed 'S' and 'LP' types are also available, and these vary from minor improvements to downright insults – and this presents a minefield for the novice.

An affordable Strat.   An affordable Les Paul.

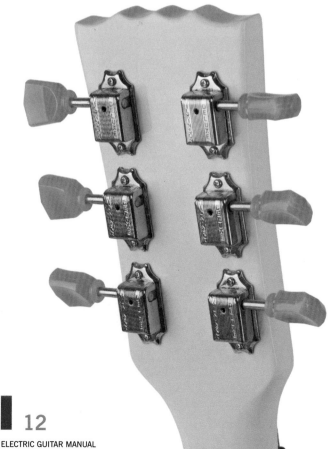

So buy where you can test-play and make an informed decision. Music shops are ideal, as they offer backup, while department stores and catalogue stores don't even know what a truss rod is, never mind where it might be adjusted. Websites offer bargain prices but are necessarily based on volume sales, not quality control or after-sales service!

Guitars are much too individual and personal to be bought like a washing machine. If possible take a teacher or a pro player with you to the retail outlet, and let him or her advise on the detail of the guitar. *Playing* the instrument is the only real way to assess its merits – and take your time, as the guitar will be your companion for the long hours of study required to achieve progression.

Other options

These days many players are drawn to the guitar but want to avoid the cliché of the familiar 'S' and 'LP' types. Up until recently this was often an expensive whim. However, Far Eastern CNC assembly brings with it a price advantage, and the range open to a beginner has never been wider. Pretty well all the classic guitar styles are now available in affordable versions: 'SGs', flying Vs and semis abound.

And it doesn't stop there – suddenly, in the early 21st century, you can buy rockabilly Gretsch lookalikes, Rickenbacker clones and retro fantasies. The only proviso is that you need to check that their beauty is more than skin-deep

A modern repro Airline.

– looking cool is fine if you're miming to a video, but live on stage you need rock-solid tuning, a resistance to acoustic feedback and good solid-sounding pickups.

One option is to buy an affordable lookalike with solid construction and then, when your budget allows, bring it up to a professional spec with quality nut, saddles and pickups. The case-study guitars in this book all offer these possibilities. One further intriguing development is the introduction of retro-style guitars that are now offered with a modern improved specification. These look cool and often work better than the originals!

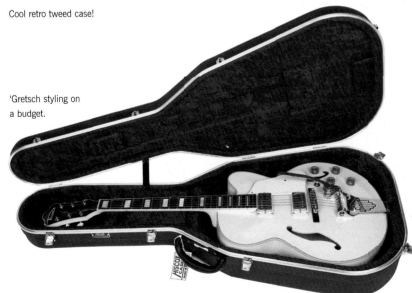

Cool retro tweed case!

'Gretsch styling on a budget.

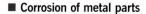

Second-hand options

Particularly in the second-hand arena, I recommend buying from a reputable dealer who'll be there next year when you need a repair or replacement, someone who you trust and can give advice on strings and other peripherals. The music industry has many trade associations, and members will display their membership in the shop; look out for that – it's your guarantee of minimum standards.

Buy from a private seller only if you know your way around the guitar and know precisely what you want. *Never* buy from an untraceable source in the proverbial back street.

Some specific issues to address include:

■ Corrosion of metal parts
Some parts of the guitar in frequent contact with sweaty palms will tend to corrode over the years, the most common area being the bridge. However, this is generally not serious. A comprehensive range of replacement parts is currently available, especially for the classic 'S', 'T', 'SG' and 'LP' types, and it seems likely that they'll remain so for the foreseeable future – one advantage of sticking to the design classics. This issue gets more complicated with the retro and wayward 'shape' guitars, where parts are harder to obtain.

■ Fret wear
A well-played guitar may need re-fretting. This is sometimes a major issue. Again, get advice and a price from an expert. Your dealer may give you a discount if you negotiate the re-fret with his in-house technicians. See page 108 for more on fretting issues.

■ Machine Heads/tuners
These can be easily replaced, but good ones aren't cheap. See page 84.

■ Pickups
Are they all working? Broken covers can easily be replaced, but pickups themselves are expensive.

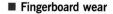

■ Fingerboard wear
This may be an issue, particularly on maple necks. However, even bad wear can be in-filled. You must weigh up the options based on how much you're attracted to the individual instrument. Again, a new neck is an option, though a premium branded one can be pricey – you may want to consider an equivalent replacement.

■ Noisy 'pots'

Tone and volume controls and switches can either be cleaned or replaced. See page 92.

■ Missing parts

Tremolo arms, pot tops and chrome 'ashtrays' are frequently missing, but they're easily replaced. Strive to replace with appropriate or even vintage repro parts. Ask for a discount!

■ Authenticity

Buyers must beware when buying a supposedly 'vintage' guitar. Fender mark their vintage reissue and relic guitars clearly. However, as a 1954 Fender Strat is currently selling for $25,000 plus, with one knob being worth $500, unscrupulous individuals may try to pass off a relatively inexpensive reissue as the priceless real thing. Serial numbers can be a useful guide (see the Fender and Gibson websites). However, even they can be faked. Only the most experienced expert can distinguish the telltale distinctions of paint finish, wear and tear, wiring details etc that identify 'the real thing'.

Verifying 'vintage' authenticity

If it were a car you were buying, you might call an automobile association for a vehicle condition check. So with a vintage guitar why not get a guitar tech to check it out? Most reputable dealers can recommend a technician with specialist knowledge of various guitars. In the end an expert guitar tech will rely as much on 'feel' in making an assessment, just as any antiques dealer would in assessing a piece of furniture.

It may seem sacrosanct to dismantle a supposedly vintage instrument. However, it's often the telltale details of vintage wiring and even solder types that distinguish the real from the repro.

Cloth shielding rather than plastic on pickup wiring is a useful clue to early guitars, but the unscrupulous will borrow such wiring from an old radio.

Seek provenance just as would an auction house such as Sotheby's or Christie's – this might include original sales documentation, hang tags, original cases, dateable photographs of the instrument in use and so on.

Laboratory paint analysis will reveal such clues as early nitro cellulose lacquer rather than modern polyurethanes. Fender and Gibson used 100% nitro cellulose paints until the late 1960s, and finishes were strictly limited. From 1969 Fenders had a catalysed undercoat and lacquer topcoat. The undercoat is often revealed in the crudely routed pickup cavities of early guitars.

The irony of all this chicanery is that it's perfectly possible today to buy a new guitar that plays better (and to my ears sometimes even sounds better) than a vintage gem. This doesn't devalue the beauty and grace of the originals one iota – just be aware that new guitars have a lot to offer.

I personally prefer my Vintage reissue '57 Strat to my first real guitar, a 1963 Fiesta Red. All the manufacturing tolerances seem more accurate on the 'new' one. Fender now has much more sophisticated computer regulated machining and as a result the new guitar stays in tune, which the vintage one sadly never did.

In the end vintage and second-hand guitars are wonderful artefacts and historical icons, but good music comes from the player's imagination and musicality as much as, if not more than, any other factor. Eric Clapton, for instance, is most frequently seen playing brand new Strats – he saves the vintage ones for recording! Vintage guitars are, in fact, less useful on stage these days as they're naturally more prone to electrical interference from the sophisticated lighting rigs, which were rare in 1954.

16

The big four

These four classic solid guitar shapes have been played by all the key players of the first half-century of rock. They have all become icons. They each have individual character that generally survives the economies imposed by cheap mass production.

'Branded' versions will all upgrade easily to a professional specification and need little more than a good set-up to see a committed player through to a first record deal. There is little point in buying an obscure lookalike when these versions are so economically priced. The exception might be makers such as Vintage, who arguably offer an upgrade on the original specification and yet remain affordable

LEFT The big four – 'LP', 'S', 'SG' and 'T' types.

RIGHT A 'Vintage' SG.

Know your
'Stratocaster' type guitar

The classic 'S' type breaks down into approximately 50 pieces. This perfectly illustrates Leo Fender's original concept of a 'parts-assembled' guitar, consistent in quality and with every component easily replaceable.

■ Double cutaways
These enable easy access to the 'dusty end of the fingerboard'. Fender guitarists soon exploited the top octave of the guitar, which had been previously difficult to access and largely neglected – one way in which Leo's invention radically changed popular music.

■ Body contours
The 'S' type was seen by Leo Fender as an improvement on his previous 'T'-type design. One notable innovation was the body contouring. Several players had complained that with Leo's previous guitar designs, such as the Broadcaster, the simple slab body could dig into your chest during a long session. Leo's response was outrageous, pragmatic, simple and effective. We now take such features totally for granted but it all started here. Jeff Beck's Esquire has DIY contours.

Originally the guitar featured 21 frets giving a top C#. This seemingly odd choice reflects the guitars 'home key' of E, which has C# as its major sixth. I suspect Leo was thinking B and then going the extra mile. Subsequent 'S' types have an added 22nd fret giving a top D – the dominant 7th in key of E.

■ Maple neck, sometimes with a rosewood fingerboard
A feature of the original concept was Leo Fender's one-piece 'disposable' neck. Many early 20th-century guitars had warped necks due to the 'new' strain of metal strings. Prior to 1920 most guitars were strung with much lower-tension gut strings. Maple and rosewood fingerboards both have their fans – but rosewood is more hardwearing.

■ Truss rod

Though reluctant at first, Leo was amongst the first to adopt a relatively accessible adjustable metal truss rod in order to rectify neck-warping problems. His radical thinking also embraced the concept of throwaway replaceable necks. The relatively narrow nut was regarded as an aid to easy playing in the days before players evolved advanced string-bending techniques.

■ Position markers

Traditional Spanish guitars have no position marker 'dots', but with the new access to the higher positions afforded on the Strat such visual clues were welcomed.

■ Body

Made of maple, ash, alder, agathis and laminates. Each wood has a subtly different effect on the acoustic sound of the 'S' type and this carries over to the amplified sound. The body is not always one-piece. Leo preferred ash to alder, and although many '50s 'S' types are one-piece Leo never insisted on this – look for *some* weight; but heavier isn't necessarily best.

■ Micro-adjustable bridge

The Stratocaster set a standard with its introduction of a bridge mechanism that allowed individual adjustment of both the height and length of each string. Ironically the precise clarity of the sound Leo achieved with his single coil pickups made this innovation a necessity, and like so many innovations it now seems obvious.

■ Tremolo/vibrato

One of the items that changed the sound of popular music. This was not the first vibrato device, but it was the first that really worked without causing too many intonation problems. Access to the 'vibrato' mechanism is usually via a rear plastic panel incorporating string-threading holes. A substantial cast trem block contributes to tone – thinner ones *sound* thinner! It's worth noting that the tremolo/vibrato arm or 'whammy bar' is supposed to be held in a suitable playing position by a tiny spring, which creates simple friction pressure on the base of the arm. This spring is often lost, as many players don't even know it's supposed to be there! It's 5/32in size. For replacements, see the *Useful contacts* appendix.

ELECTRIC GUITAR MANUAL

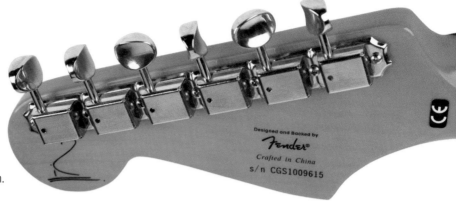

■ Recessed jack socket

Yet another innovation, much easier to handle than the edge-fixed socket on the 'T' type and 1951 Precision bass. This meant extensive design work and retooling – not a cheap option. Cheaper 'S' types often lack this feature.

■ Four-bolt neck

This simple design was briefly compromised during the much-maligned period when CBS owned Fender in the mid '60s. However, Jimi Hendrix coaxed many a good tune out of CBS Fenders with three-bolt necks.

■ Strap button

You don't really sit down to play a Strat – this guitar was designed for 'Western Swing'. Look out for poorly fitted screws!

■ String guide

A simple design that improves the engagement of the strings at the guitar nut. This innovation has undergone several redesigns.

■ Volume and tone potentiometers

Resistive capacitor circuits. A simple arrangement familiar to Leo from his days repairing radios. The resistive capacitor circuit de-emphasises selected frequencies in the pickup circuit of the middle and neck pickups. Cheap tiny pots are a false economy.

■ Three pickups

These are a refinement on Leo's 'T'-type design. The pickups feature 'harmonic positioning'. The neck pickup is positioned at a point where it will most emphasise the fundamental harmonic, the bridge pickup to most emphasise the higher order harmonics. The middle pickup sits between the two. Cheap versions have ceramic rather than alnico magnets and may have a bar magnet doing the work.

■ Enclosed machine heads

Not a first but still quite novel. Enclosed machines were in fact known in the 19th century, but they became more of a necessity in the gritty environment of Texas hoedowns. Leo was wholly practical. He didn't make his own initially but bought them in from the specialist Kluson company. These days 'S' types have a varied range of tuners.

■ Single-row machines

Having the machines on the player's side of the neck in a single accessible row is again not a first but another example of Leo and his team pulling together the best design concepts in one instrument.

■ Pickguard

Single-ply plastic or anodised metal pickguard and electronics mount. An innovation which Leo enjoyed, as this meant all the guitar's electrics were assembled as a one-piece single-mount component. From about 1959 the single-ply was replaced by a triple-ply assembly that was less inclined to warping and cracking. The new fingerboard sometimes incorporated a metal layer intended to improve electronic screening. The two fingerboards are not interchangeable, due to an eight-screw assembly becoming eleven-screw for the laminated version.
.

More detailed specific screening information and maintenance notes are to be found in Haynes' *Fender Stratocaster Manual*.

■ Three-way pickup selector switch

Leo was quite content with this three-position switch and objected to what he called the 'snarl' effect of the combinations of 'S'-type pickups. However, players soon made devious use of matchsticks jammed in the socket groove to achieve such ear-tingling 'phase' effects. Cheap PCB types often fail.

Know your
'Les Paul' type guitar

The second most popular type of solid-body electric guitar is based on the Gibson Les Paul 'Standard' of circa 1959–60. Many copies are supplied in a black finish that alludes to the 'Black Beauty' guitar but neatly skirts the critical issue of a figured maple top, and often disguises inferior wood.

■ **Tune-O-Matic bridge and stop tail**
By 1957 the Les Paul had evolved a stable bridge arrangement with adequate scope for adjustment, and most 'LP' types have some variant of this.

■ **Humbucking pickups**
Though not the first Gibson guitar to have Seth Lover's revolutionary humbuckers, the 'LP' is the guitar that has most come to define their classic sound. One of the weakest links on copy 'LPs' are inferior pickups – some are actually single coils in a humbucker case!

■ **Richly figured maple**
One of critical factors in a collector's valuation of a 'Standard' is the quality and intensity of the figured grain in the carved and matched maple top – Epiphone sometimes compromise by offering a veneered maple top rather than a plain maple cap to a mahogany base.

■ **'Florentine' cutaway**
By the standards of the late 1950s this gave generous access to the higher frets. The 'Regular' or Standard has 22 frets, giving the played top D the minor 7th in the guitar's home key of E. The fret gauge is in the range 2.4–2.68mm.

■ **24¾in-scale fully bound mahogany neck**
With rosewood fingerboard and often trapezoid position
markers. Mahogany for stability – watch out for wobbly soft woods.
The neck should also be glued, not bolted, for a true 'LP' sound.

■ **Strap button**
Located on the
top bout – the
'LP' is designed
to be played
standing up.
Boots on the
front stage
monitor optional.

■ **Three-a-side headstock**
A traditional headstock found on
guitars dating back to the 1920s, usually
with a shield-type cover to the truss rod access.

■ **Enclosed machines**
Klusons were the natural choice for early Standard 'LPs' and
are now replaced by lookalikes or modern Grovers for current
models, with better wind ratios and better internal components.

■ **Headstock pitch**
The original 'LPs' had a 17° pitch – Gibsons' long experience
as luthiers meant no need for string trees. The pressure at
the nut also aids a natural acoustic sustain. Most copies
have a much shallower pitch; ensure that the strings are well
secured in the nut. Ideally the 'LP' has a 'long tenon' fixed
neck. This and the shorter scale, coupled with some PAF-
type humbuckers, are the heart of the classic 'LP' sound.

■ **Fingerboard with traditional
fairly flat radius of 12in**
The flatter radius of the
'LP' Standard was ironically
unfashionable by 1958 but
found its fans as the Blues
Boom guitarists of the late
'60s discovered that this
flatter profile lends itself
to choke-free string
'bends'.

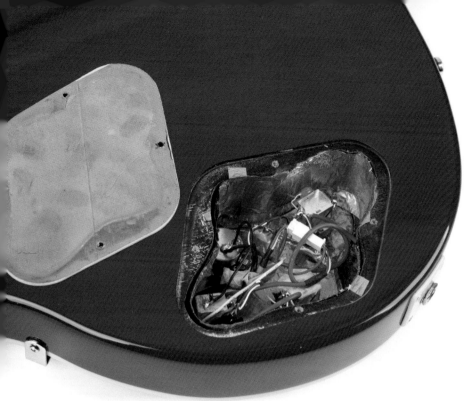

■ **Jack output socket**
Primitive, simple, effective. Not particularly elegant, but it does the job. Look out for intermittent and loose connections.

■ **Easy-access electrics**
A touch of genius here, as all the electrical controls can be accessed by removing a few Phillips screws. No need to de-string or remove a mass of screws in an emergency repair. In researching his guitar Les Paul had availed himself of some earlier Epiphone archtops that featured a rear trapdoor for electrical access, but this was a first on a professional class solid guitar. Look out for tiny and usually inferior pots. All the controls and associated capacitors are easily replaced or cleaned.

■ **Paired volume and tone controls**
Non-fussy
on-stage access.

■ **A separate pickguard**
A traditional approach, as previously used on Gibson's archtops. The guard floats off the guitar, thereby not impeding sustain. It is also removable if desired, for better appearance and a clearer picking space. Some Standards are now supplied without a pickguard, the better to show the 'burst top.

■ **Clear picking space**
The Standard always had two pickups, each distinct in their roles at picking up a different sample of string harmonics. This approach also leaves a useful clear picking space between pickups. Some copies ape the 3PU custom, adding unnecessary flash and weight.

For more on the 'LP' guitar and very specific model information see Haynes' *Gibson Les Paul Manual*.

■ **Pickup selector**
Robust and easily accessible, the switch needs a special tool for safe (*ie* no-scratch) removal but is otherwise a good, simple, performance-friendly design. Often economised on copies – easily replaced, however.

Know your
'Telecaster' type guitar

In 1950 Leo Fender combined everything the electric guitarist needed in this simple workmanlike design: a rigid platform, simple but effective electrics and great playability.

■ **Body**

Prototyped originally in pine, the Esquire/Broadcaster/Tele was finally production made in ash, though it has since been made of alder, rosewood, basswood and a number of exotic hybrids. A recent 'Vintage Vibe' Tele from Squier returned to pine and sounds fine – anything reasonably dense is going to provide the necessary rigid platform. Thinline semi-hollow 'T' types are lighter but somehow retain the classic twang.

■ **Pickguard**

Plastics are now the practical norm but if you want authentic Bakelite these are available as retro fits.

■ **Integral bridge and pickup**

The heart of the 'T' type is surely this almost unique combination unit. The position of the pickup and its oneness with the semi-compensated and adjustable bridge make for a sound that remains unmistakable. Brass saddles with two strings per unit are the serious Tele players' first choice, though six-saddle versions are easier to intonate. 'Through-body' stringing is a sustain-enhancing essential.

■ **Neck-body join**

You need a good snug fit – accurately cut, and correctly aligned with the bridge.

■ **Neck**

A fine piece of maple, straight and strong with accurate frets. Rosewood is a more sensible choice for a fingerboard if the guitar is going to be heavily gigged.

■ Truss rod
A modern headstock
end adjustment makes
a lot of practical sense.

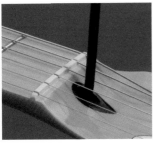

**■ Jack
socket**
I would
look for a
screwed-in
Electrosocket
arrangement
for sheer
practicality.

■ Pickup selector
This needs to be a rugged
design, and if your guitar
comes with a frail PCB type
then consider a swift upgrade.
If in use it 'clicks' electrically it
will also cause unpredictable
earthing problems, so ask for
a decent one at purchase –
fitting is relatively simple.

■ Machine heads
Modern machine heads make
for better stability, though there
are some very good recent
Klusons that maintain the
'cool retro' look.

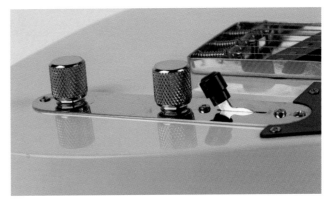

■ Neck pickup
Go for a useful modern pickup
in the traditional design for
a useable optional tone.

For very specific information on pickups
and modifications see Haynes' *Fender
Telecaster Manual*.

Know your
'SG' type guitar

A 1960 evolution from
the Les Paul Junior and
'Melody Maker', this
was Gibson's futuristic
response to the
Stratocaster – two
cutaways, contoured
and light, but with all the
might of the Seth Lover PAF
humbucker pickup. This tribute
is from the manufacturer Vintage.

■ **Body**
An ultra-thin and light contoured body, ideally one piece of
walnut or mahogany with unprecedented access to all the
higher frets – sometimes even a full two octaves on every string.

■ **Neck**
Very slim – so slim and unsupported
that it's liable to wobble even on
Gibsons – this put Les Paul off, and
he had his name removed.
Check before you buy!
They always wobble,
but the good 'SET'
glued necks are under
sufficient control. Avoid
a bolt-on neck on an
'SG' type. Jaydee
Custom Guitars will
do you a 'through
neck' version where
the neck and body
are fully integrated.

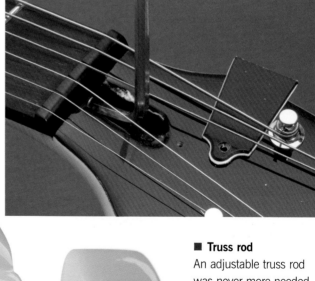

■ **Truss rod**
An adjustable truss rod
was never more needed.

Selector
A rugged three-way selector. Easily replaced if this is supplied as a flimsy import.

Volume and tone potentiometers
Two tones, two volumes – cheap tiny pots are easily upgraded.

Humbucking pickups
Two or three humbuckers (check that these *really are* humbuckers, as many imported 'SG' types are sold with pickup cans containing budget single coils!). These are Trev Wilkinson's, and will deliver!

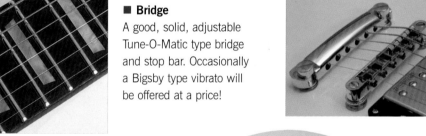

Fingerboard
A flattish fingerboard – ideal for 'string-bending' rock and blues.

Machine heads
Three-a-side tuners – Klusons for authenticity and lightness (balance can be critical on this neck-centric guitar).

Bridge
A good, solid, adjustable Tune-O-Matic type bridge and stop bar. Occasionally a Bigsby type vibrato will be offered at a price!

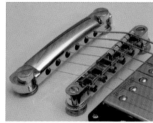

Trapdoor
This useful access port is a carry-over from Les Paul's Archtop Epiphones and his '52 Les Paul, which also had trapdoors in the back – Les Paul liked to tinker, and why not?

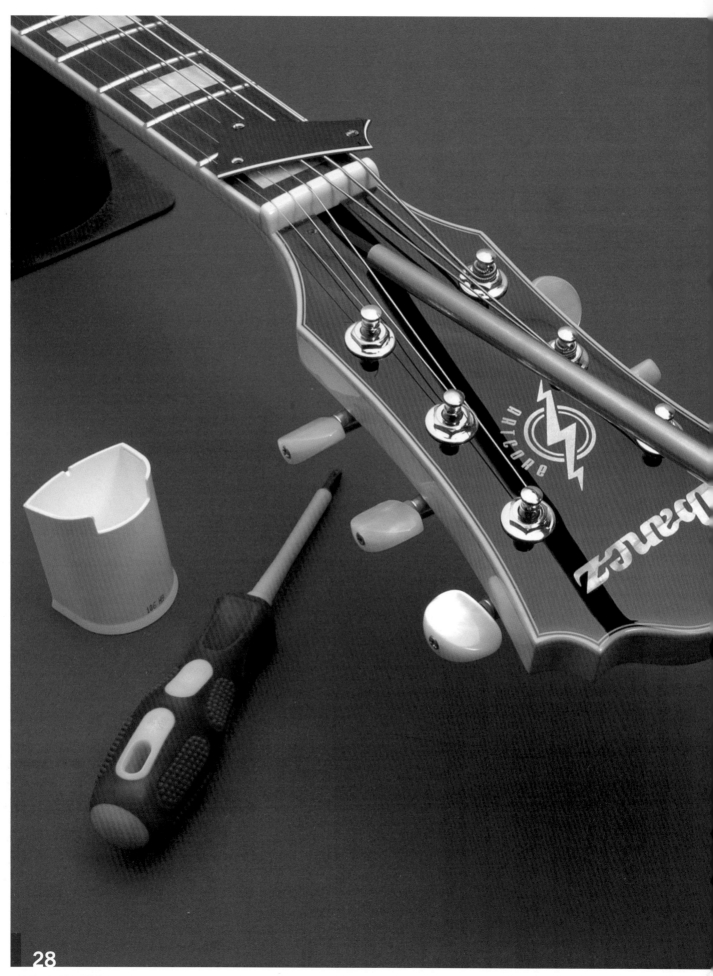

Getting started

If you're very lucky your guitar will arrive home perfectly set up, but this is very rare, and – naturally – most aspiring guitarists find it hard to know what to assess.

Start by getting the guitar in tune and then try a first simple chord. Then play it again *louder*!

LEFT A 1/4 turn on the truss rod.

RIGHT Danelectro '63 re-issue.

Tuning and your first 'power chord'

At this point you should ideally get some guidance from an expert, somebody with guitar experience; but if you're on your own, *try to get the guitar in tune*.

Don't leave the shop without a tuner.

Many guitar 'kits' come with a free tuner – don't forget the battery!

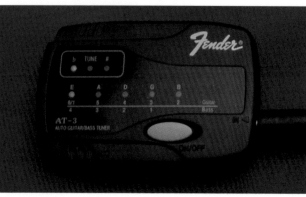

Sadly, guitar strings will tend to go out of tune – this is normal, as temperature changes and the knocks and vibration of travel have had their affect on the critical string tension. Many new guitars arrive by freight from the other side of the world, and their tuning will essentially be radically out. However, even the trip from your local music shop to your home is enough to cause microtonal errors.

Nothing sounds worse than an out-of-tune instrument, and tuning guitars used to be a complicated skill that could only be acquired by trial and error. However, the advent of cheap electronic tuners has made the prospect a lot less daunting.

1 Plug the guitar into your tuner with a simple jack to jack guitar lead. Turn the tuner on and select/calibrate A440 as the target pitch (if you're offered no option then this will be the preset).

2 Turn the guitar volume up full and select the neck pickup. Turn the tone control fully anticlockwise. This all helps the tuner 'home in' on the fundamental note of the guitar's open or 'unfretted' strings.

Play the lowest/thickest string, which in conventional tuning should be an E.

The tuner should detect this pitch and light up or indicate sharp or flat. How this is indicated varies. A meter-type tuner will indicate sharp or flat on a display scale: flat is usually 'Low' on the meter and sharp is 'High', indicating the note is too low or too high – logical enough? 'In tune' corresponds to '0' or the 12:00pm position. Other types of tuner have a series of LEDs that perform the same function.

3 If the lowest string is *not* close to E the tuner will usually display the note it's nearest to in the alphabet – *eg* D if it's very flat (too low) or F if the note is very sharp (too high).

After a string-change or a long journey the string will occasionally be way off pitch, most often far too low; say C instead of E:

ABCDEFGABCD

The tuner will usually detect this and tell you on the display by lighting up the incorrect pitch.

If this happens:

1 Slowly tension the string with the tuning peg nearest your left hand (assuming you're playing a right-handed guitar).

2 The guitar tuner display should now move up through the alphabet:

ABCDEFGABCD

3 Keep slowly tensioning the string until you hit the target E, and then fine-tune so that this note is a correct E as indicated by the tuner's meter.

Now perform the same procedure for the other five strings.

This *won't* be easy initially, but it gets easier with repetition and you'll gradually learn to hear the flatness or sharpness of the notes and be able to adjust accordingly.

NB: If the guitar is difficult to get in tune this often highlights the need for a set-up.

If you *can* get the guitar in tune, *have some fun!*

Turn the guitar amplifier volume down to zero and plug the output of the guitar into the amps input using a simple jack to jack guitar cable. Now turn up the volume.

Have a good *Kerrang!* – you could try a simple one-finger E power chord, with lots of gain and a bit of 'whammy' where available!

In the diagram below the strings are marked vertically and the frets horizontally. EBE are the notes sounded and the XXX means 'not played'.

The figure '1' on the black dots refers to your left hand first finger, as shown in the photo. The 'open' E and the first finger alone will also give a simpler power chord.

E Power Chord

	E	B	E	X	X	X
1						
		①		①		
3						
5						frets

Simplified version

	O	X	X	X	X	X
1						
			①			
3						
5						frets

A mini 'pod' and headphones for hassle-free practice.

Some of the available 'starter kit' guitars come with their own DVD for some useful visual guides to this.

A drum machine such as those built into some inexpensive multi-FX units, playing a simple four-beat groove and plugged into the amps input, makes this first simple chord a lot more fun!

Another alternative is a CD or MP3 player with 'drum trax' plugged into the amps AUX input (or any other second input).

Play it again! If you have valued neighbours then get an amp which has a headphones output – most of the small multi-FX units recommended on page 113 also have this facility.

WIth that out of your system, let's get your guitar properly on the road.

Getting your guitar working properly

The importance of accurate tuning and a good set-up are particularly crucial when you begin learning to play the guitar. Let nobody tell you otherwise! You'll simply give up learning if you get too many calluses and the guitar still sounds naff. Never think, or allow a salesman to tell you, that 'It's OK for now!' With the early stages of learning physically the hardest and the most crucial, you need a decent set up NOW! Experienced players can get a tune out of anything, but at start-up you need all the help you can get.

LEFT Setting the intonation.

RIGHT A Squier Strat.

A string change and plastic film removal

I strongly recommend that on most new guitars you quickly change the strings for some professional 009-042 D'Addarios or strings of equivalent quality – these will tune and *stay* in tune better than cheap factory-fitted strings, and their light gauge will save you some strain on your unexercised digits!

Whenever possible change one string at a time to avoid drastic changes in tension on the neck and any vibrato assembly.

You should also remove any factory-fitted plastic protective film. This is best taken off with the knobs and pickguard screws removed. Any push-fit knobs often come off with a duster threaded under the skirt, and the screws by means of a No '1' Phillips screwdriver.

If necessary the volume and tone pots will often come off using a 10mm socket wrench – the protective polythene otherwise becomes stuck under the screws and creates a dust-accumulating mess. Back panels also often have a layer of protective film, and sometimes even the pickups.

A note on strings

You should change these according to use – at least monthly if you're gigging and at least every three months if you're a learner. Use the same brand consistently, and use the same gauge and metal type, as this will save time-consuming adjustments to the action and intonation. Different strings have different tensions, and gauges can vary from heavy to extra light. Cheap strings are a generally a false economy as they're inconsistent and wear out quicker.

A good benchmark in stringing modern 'S' or 'T' types is .009 (first) to .042 (sixth) – light gauge strings for flexibility, but not too light. Experiment around this area for your own sound. Hank Marvin of British group The Shadows achieved his distinctive early sound with much heavier strings – but that was in an era before much 'string bending' activity.

More recently Stevie Ray Vaughan has used heavier strings to achieve a distinctive tone (he managed to 'bend' his heavy strings by tuning them below standard concert pitch). Some heavy metal and 'shred' guitarists use strings lighter than .009. Experiment, but refer to the set-up information that follows to ensure your guitar is adjusted to cope.

New strings are consistent in their profile and hence more harmonically correct along their length – this makes them easier to tune. Old strings are worn by fret contact, inconsistent, and above all sound dull.

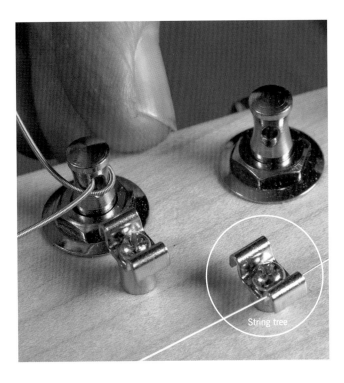

String tree

Keep new strings sounding good longer by wiping them with a lint-free cloth after every use. This removes corrosive perspiration and prevents premature rusting.

Today's fashionable guitar sounds tend to be bright and crisp and this is best achieved with conventional roundwound strings, usually made of nickel wound on steel. Stainless steel is another long-lasting option, though beware of using strings that are made of a material harder than your frets, as inevitably this will result in quicker fret wear.

'Coated strings' are more resistant to corrosion, though are initially more expensive.

Always use *electric guitar* strings. This sounds obvious, but acoustic guitar strings aren't designed for magnetic pickups and therefore aren't always magnetically consistent – electric guitar strings are! Stick to one brand, especially if you're changing individual strings, as these will be balanced across the gauges both physically and magnetically.

To reduce string breakage lightly lubricate the string/saddle contact point sparingly with a light machine oil (3-in-1 oil contains anti-rust and anti-corrosive properties). Do this every time you change your strings. The oil acts as an insulator against moisture, and reduces friction and metal fatigue.

Another area that should be lubricated is the string tree(s). A small amount of ChapStick or Lubrikit, applied with a matchstick, will suffice.

Stringing an 'S' or 'T' type guitar – vintage keys
These feature a unique slotted barrel.

One obstacle to changing vintage 'S'-type strings is the 'thru body' stringing. However, if the vibrato is aligned properly then it shouldn't be too difficult – the vibrato block holes should line up with the holes in the plastic backplate (see 'S'-type trem alignment, page 48).

■ When removing old strings, cutting off the curly ends will assist their passage through the trem block.

1 When possible always change one string at a time to avoid drastic changes in tension on the neck and vibrato assembly. Due to the unique vintage design you'll need to pre-cut the strings to achieve the proper length and the desired amount of winds. Starting with the sixth string, first pull the new sixth string (taking up any slack) to the fourth string key (this will give you enough length for the windings – see above).

2 Bend and crimp the string to a 90° angle and cut it to length.

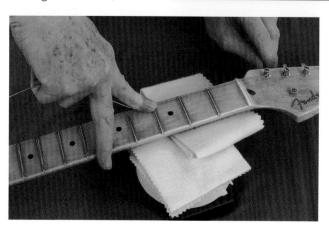

3 Insert the string into the centre hole in the tuning key, and wind neatly in a downward pattern – carefully, so as to prevent overlapping the windings. Keep the string under tension with your fingers.

4 Repeat the procedure as above, *ie* pull the fifth string to the third key and cut and tension it. Then pull the fourth string between the second and first keys and cut it. Pull the third string just about to the top of the headstock and cut it. Pull the second string about a 0.5in (13mm) past the headstock and cut it. Finally, pull the first string 1.5in (38mm) past the top of the headstock and cut it.

Stringing an 'S' or 'T' type guitar – standard keys

Many 'modern' 'S' types have a conventional horizontal hole in the machine-head barrel.

NB: If your tuning keys have a screw on the end of the button, check the tightness of the screw, as this controls the tension of the gears inside the tuning keys. You should slacken this tension for ease of restringing. After stringing it is very important not to over-tighten these screws. They should be tightened only 'finger-tight'. This is particularly important on locking tuners.

1 In order to reduce string slippage at the tuning key, I recommend that you use a tie technique. This is accomplished by pulling the string through the keyhole, then pulling it clockwise underneath itself and bringing it back over the top of itself, creating a knot.

This is done under tension and achieves a situation with very few turnings on the machine-head barrel. This is particularly desirable when extensive use is made of the trem/ vibrato – less windings mean less 'unwindings' as the trem is depressed and the string tension reduced.

You'll need to leave a bit of slack for the first string, so you have perhaps two to three winds around the post. As you progress down the line to the sixth string you'll reduce the amount of slack and the amount of winds around the keys.

2 Tighten the string under tension as right.

3 Crimp any excess string with wire cutters.

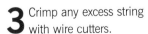

Tech Tip

I find a 'cake tester', available from cookery shops, makes the deal tool for dislodging any strings jammed in trem blocks.

John Diggins – Luthier

Fender recommendations

For tuning stability Fender recommend Fender Bullet strings.

The patented bullet-end is specifically designed for all styles of Fender tremolo/vibrato use, from extreme 'dives' to smooth vibrato passages. The design allows the string to travel freely in the bridge block channel during tremolo use and return afterwards to its original position, seated snugly in the bridge block. This is accomplished by eliminating the extra string wrap and the ball-end (a conventional ball-end doesn't quite fit properly in the Strat string channel). The 'bullet-end' has been shaped and sized to precisely match the design of the bridge block channel.

However, the bullets – and indeed, sometimes conventional 'ball ends' too – can become lodged in their sockets in the trem block (see Tech Tip above).

Stringing an 'LP' or semi-acoustic guitar with a stop tail bridge

■ If your tuning keys have a screw on the end of the button as with most Grovers, check the tightness of the screw, as this controls the tension of the gears inside the tuning keys. You should slacken this tension for ease of restringing.

■ As a rule you should change strings one at a time, maintaining an even tension on the neck and thus avoiding any movement in the neck angle.

■ When removing old strings, cutting off the curly ends will assist their passage through the stop tail bridge.

1 Thread the new string through the stop tail and insert it into the centre hole in the tuning key.

2 In order to reduce string slippage at the tuning key, I recommend that you use a tie technique. This is accomplished by pulling the string through the keyhole, then pulling the string clockwise underneath itself and bringing it back over the top of itself, creating a knot.

Do this under tension and leave just enough string to achieve a few turnings on the machine-head barrel. Wind neatly in a downward pattern – carefully, so as to prevent overlapping the windings. Keep the string under tension with your fingers.

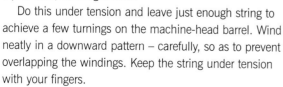

3 Repeat the procedure as above. Note that the bass strings on the left side of the headstock require a clockwise tie and the treble three strings on the right side require an anticlockwise tie. Crimp any excess string with wire cutters.

String stretching

To avoid slippage stretch your strings properly. Having installed a new set and tuned them to pitch, hold the strings at the first fret and hook your fingers under each string (one at a time) and tug lightly, moving your hand from the bridge to the neck. Retune the guitar and repeat this process several times.

Truss rod adjustment

The introduction of the adjustable metal truss rod by Gibson's Thaddeus McHugh in 1921 enabled accurate setting of the required 'relief' in the guitar's fretboard.

Setting the correct neck relief

With a new set of light gauge strings set at normal A440 pitch, the neck of an electric guitar should be *almost* straight, but with a small concave tendency that allows the strings to vibrate freely – this is referred to as 'relief'.

The original Gibson concept of the truss rod – a metal spoke set into the neck – was to discourage the wooden neck from overbending under the stress of string tension. The added advantage of the modern truss rod is the possibility of readjustment, effected by tightening a pre-bent rod or rods and thereby straightening an over-bent neck.

Vintage-style 'S' types, some Danelectros and many other solid bolt-on neck guitars

This Standard type of truss rod adjusts at the heel of the neck, which is often difficult to access. It can counteract concave curvature, for example in a neck that has too much relief, by generating a force in the neck opposite to that caused by excessive string tension.

1 Check your tuning (which should be at standard A440 pitch or your preferred and consistent 'custom pitch'). Next we need to check the neck for relief – is it straight, or bowed either convex or concave? Install a capo at the 1st fret, depress the sixth string at the last fret.

✏ **Tech Tip**

You can loosen the strings a little and then undo the two back neck screws. This then enables you to tip the neck up enough to reach the rod screw. But I don't usually do this in front of the client – it looks horrendous!

Andy Gibson – Luthier

2 With a feeler gauge, check the gap between the bottom of the string and the top of the 8th fret. See the specification chart below for the correct gap. This will vary depending on the radius of your particular neck type.

If neck is too concave (indicated by too big a gap measured with the feeler gauge) then you may consider adjusting the truss rod.

Do NOT do this on a rare and precious guitar if you feel unqualified. Talk instead to an experienced guitar tech via your local music shop.

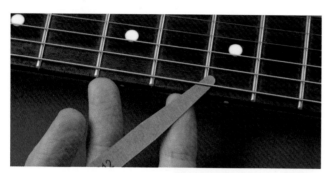

3 Slacken the strings. Then, using a No '2' Phillips screwdriver carefully unscrew the four neck bolts approximately 1/8in at the top and 1in at the 'back' – this should be enough to tilt the neck back for access to the truss rod screw.

NB: Be very careful to note the position of any neck shims (small slivers of wood or card in the neck pocket), as they must remain in the same position when the neck is reseated.

Access to the truss rod on vintage and reissue '50s and '60s 'S' types varies, as some have a small cut-out indentation in the pickguard to enable easier access. Generally the earliest guitars and their reissues do not have this. With these guitars you may have to unscrew the neck bolts slightly more to access the truss rod and avoid the risk of damaging the pickguard.

4 Adjust the truss rod screw a quarter-turn clockwise.
NB: Although this is really a job for a straight-slot 8mm or 11/32in screwdriver, with the difficult access involved a No '2' Phillips works well and risks less damage to the plastic pickguard.

5 Alternatively, if the neck is too convex (strings too close to the fingerboard), turn the truss rod nut a quarter turn anti-clockwise to allow the string tension to pull more relief into the neck.

NB: For obvious reasons the vintage truss rod was originally conceived to adjust situations with too much relief – it is much more likely to be successful in this application.

6 Checking that any shims are correctly reseated, replace the neck and re-tension the strings to correct pitch.

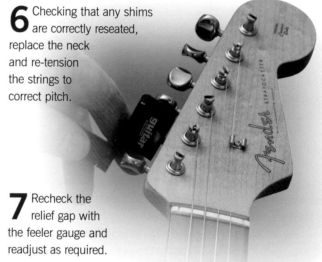

7 Recheck the relief gap with the feeler gauge and readjust as required.

NB: In either case, if you meet excessive resistance when adjusting the truss rod, or your instrument needs constant adjustment, or adjusting the truss rod has no effect on the neck, take your instrument to a local guitar tech via your local musical instrument shop.

Recommended neck relief

Neck radius	Relief
7.25in	.012in (0.3mm)
9.5in to 12in	.010in (0.25mm)
15in to 17in	.008in (0.2mm)

NB: You may need to reset the individual string height following truss rod adjustment.

The 'Bi-Flex' truss rod system

There are two types of Standard truss rod: the type that adjusts at the heel of the neck, as described above, and another type that adjusts at the headstock. Later 'S' types and some other modern electric and acoustic guitars have the latter variety, which includes the Bi-Flex system.

The Bi-Flex Truss Rod (used on most American Fender and American Deluxe Series 'S'-type and 'T'-type instruments) was designed by Fender in the early 1980s. Unlike most truss rods, which can only correct a neck that is too concave (under-bowed), the Bi-Flex truss rod can compensate for either concave or convex (over-bowed) curvature, by generating a force in either direction as needed.

Tightened as usual the truss rod nut bows the neck backwards. As you loosen the nut you'll find the neck's neutral. If you continue to loosen the nut you'll feel a renewed tightening as the rod pushes against a walnut dowel, causing the neck to bow forward.

1 Check your tuning (which should be at standard A440 pitch or your preferred and consistent 'custom pitch'). Install a capo at the 1st fret, depress the sixth string at the last fret.

2 With a feeler gauge, check the gap between the bottom of the string and the top of the 8th fret. See the specification chart on page 42 for the correct gap. This will vary depending on the radius of your particular neck type.

If the neck is too concave (indicated by too big a gap measured with the feeler gauge) then you may consider adjusting the truss rod.

See the specification chart on page 42 for the correct gap.

Tech Tip

This adjustment also applies to 'LP' and 'SG' types.

3 Adjustment at headstock (NB: Allen key sizes vary depending on the model and date, refer to the case studies in this manual for guidance).

First sight down the edge of the fingerboard from behind the headstock, looking toward the body of the instrument.

4 Turn the truss rod nut clockwise to remove excess relief. If the neck is too convex (strings too close to the fingerboard), turn the truss rod nut anticlockwise to allow the string tension to pull more relief into the neck.

5 Check your tuning, then recheck the gap with the feeler gauge and readjust as necessary.

NB: In either case, if you meet excessive resistance when adjusting the truss rod, or your instrument seems to need constant adjustment, or adjusting the truss rod has no effect on the neck, then take the instrument to a qualified guitar tech.

Nut adjustment or replacement

Having checked and adjusted the neck relief, next check the nut.
This small piece of bone, metal, plastic or ebony has a decisive
effect on how any guitar performs.

Too high?

On 90% of new guitars the nut arrives set too high.
This causes the action of the guitar to be too difficult for first
position chords and, more importantly, upsets the intonation
of the fretting, causing first position notes to fret sharp. A good
indicator of nut problems is to place a capo at the 1st fret: if
the guitar now feels easier to play and sounds more in tune
then the nut is probably too high.

Filing nut slots to the correct depth isn't easy and ideally
requires a set of gauged nut files. However, a cheap plastic nut
can often be improved with some inexpensive needle files and a
little patient experimentation. Always mask the surrounding guitar
surfaces and take care not to overdo the width and depth of the
nut slots – a feeler gauge set to approximate the intended depth
makes a good safety stop. You need to allow for the fret height
and the string height with a margin for the strings' excursion,
allowing more on the bass strings due to their thicker gauge.
You'll also need to take into account
the fingerboard radius.

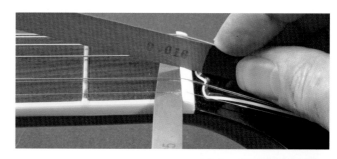

An alternative is to carefully
remove the nut (see below) and
simply file a small amount of
plastic from the base – I find
it easier to keep the bottom of
the nut flat by putting the file
in a vice and abrading the nut
against this, with a guide line
etched into the nut surface. I
then reglue the nut in position.

Too low?

Rarely the nut is too low causing open played strings to snag
on the frets and 'buzz'. A simple temporary solution is a small
shim of wood in the nut slot – raising the nut a fraction and
often solving the immediate problem.

Replacing a nut

NB: Below is a nut replacement procedure for an 'LP'/'SG' and
most electric guitars – though 'S' and 'T' type guitars have
an enclosed nut slot; the procedure is otherwise the same.

■ So why would you want to do this adjustment?

Wear in the nut slots perhaps caused by the sawing action of
extensive vibrato use or just tuning and wear and tear, can make the
'action' at the nut/1st fret too low, resulting in buzzing and snagging.

Another reason is to perhaps replace a cheap plastic nut with
a bone substitute, which has better acoustic properties and
is self-lubricating.

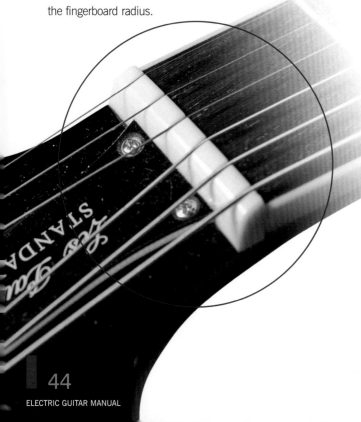

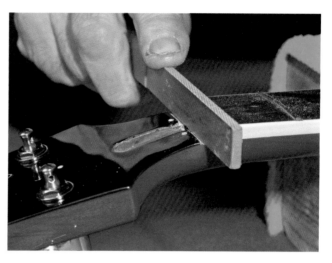

Tools required

- Small hammer
- Feeler gauges
- Specialist precision nut-shaping files in the correct gauges for your strings
- Smooth-ended pliers
- Specialist nut-seating file
- A sharp craft knife
- A sharp chisel, custom width slightly less than 1/8in
- X-ACTO or equivalent razor saws

1 Remove the strings. Be aware of any loose bridge and tailpiece, which can be secured with a couple of rubber bands. There's usually no overlapping polyurethane on an 'LP' type, so just remove the truss rod cover with a No '1' Phillips screwdriver. If you're not a skilled luthier I would recommend protecting the fingerboard and head-stock with several layers of protective masking tape.

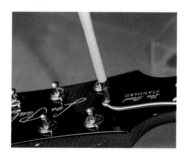

2 Remove the old nut. Tap the nut gently using a small hammer. With luck the nut should eventually become loose and can be removed as one piece reasonably easily. As a last resort prise the nut out with a pair of smooth-ended pliers. The smooth ends will avoid damaging the old nut, which – assuming you were happy with your original string spacing – provides a perfect template for the new spacing.

3 If necessary, clean the nut slot of any surplus adhesive, lacquer etc. A narrow and sharp file can be used as an effective tool on both the end of the fingerboard and the bottom of the nut slot. A custom file slightly narrower than 1/8in is required.

4 It's important to avoid chipping the neck finish, so gently file the sharp edge of any lacquer and also file the nut bottom with inward strokes from both ends of the nut slot, thus avoiding accidentally pulling any lacquer from the neck.

5 Approximate the new nut blank. Begin with an oversize blank, which can then be shaped down to a custom fit. A bench grinder will save a lot of time.

A word of warning

The nut is one of the most difficult and skilled adjustment/ replacements for an amateur. Correct nut shaping – which is essential to ensure stable tuning, good tone and correct string spacing – is not a job to be taken lightly. Even if you're buying a pre-formed nut you'll need specialist tools to make minor adjustments. If you're at all unsure of your skills or tooling then I recommend you take your guitar to a qualified guitar tech or luthier.

6 Measure your nut slot width and mark the required nut slots on your new blank based on the precise measurements of your nut slot and your old nut. Ideally you should carefully copy the string spacing from the old nut. Pay particular attention to the spacing of the sixth and first strings from the outside edge. Having strings too close to the edge will make finger vibrato difficult.

> ### ✏ Tech Tip
>
> **Bone has the advantage of being self-lubricating.**
>
> *John Diggins – Luthier*

■ Check constantly for a snug and even fit in the nut slot. At this juncture the nut should still be left slightly overlong for flexibility at the later stages of shaping. A 1/8in edge overlap will be enough to allow for some fine-tuning.

7 Draw the fingerboard outline radius on to the new nut with a sharp pencil.

Emergency measures

An alternative to a complete nut replacement, and useful in an emergency – especially if only one or two nut slots are too deep – is to recycle some material from the top of the nut (assuming excess is available) and use this as infilling material.

To do this, tape both sides of the nut with masking tape, then take a coarse file and file the top of the nut approximately half the depth you expect to raise the slots. Catch the loose filings on a piece of paper. Fill the offending slots with the loose filings. Then carefully soak the filings with thin superglue. Press the solution into place with a toothpick. When dry, re-file the slots, referring to the methods described above. As before, the slots should be made so the string sits in them to about half to three-quarters of its diameter, though a Les Paul will cope quite well with deeper nut slots, especially if you're a 'heavy picker'. Slots should taper downwards on the tuner side and again the strings' first point of contact must be at the fret side of the nut.

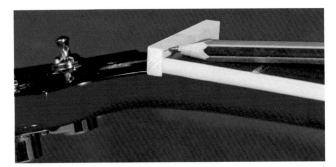

8 Add a pencil radius above the fingerboard outline. This new radius needs to be enough to account for the fret height, the string height and the thickness of the string (a guitar tech might add a little more for good measure!). You will certainly need to allow a little more height towards the bass strings, as they need more room to vibrate without 'choking' on the first fret.

9 You can position the first two outer strings on the new nut by making pilot notches with a very fine craft saw (X-ACTO or similar, with a blade of .010 gauge or less). If for some reason you do not have the old nut then a specialist tool, a compensated nut spacing template, is the easiest way to get even spacing between the outside of adjoining strings – a more important factor than equal spacing at their centres. Use this or the old nut to determine the position of the remaining string slots.

■ Surprising as it might seem, expert luthiers often determine the individual string spacing by eye. Though this sounds a little unscientific, the precise calculations in thousandths of an inch are made very complex by the fact that each string is a different gauge. (This is where the template can be used for reference.)

■ You can adopt the pro method to a degree by positioning the strings in very shallow 'pilot' slots and then making any minor adjustments by eye before completing your filing of the final slots.

10 Carefully file the new slots to the depth marked on the new nut. In practice this can be 'fine-tuned' on the guitar.

Specialist precision nut files will allow smoothing of the nut slot bottom without damaging the sides of the slot (See *Useful contacts* appendix). These files have smooth edges and a round bottom and are available in the precise size for your chosen string gauges. In practice a luthier would use a slightly smaller file than the requisite slot and use a rolling technique on the forward motion to widen the slot with more control and less chance of the file snagging. A carefully chosen feeler gauge can be a useful guide whilst filing, preventing any chance of filing too deep. The correct depth for the string slots – which as a rule is slightly more than the fret height – is calculated using a feeler gauge and a straight edge.

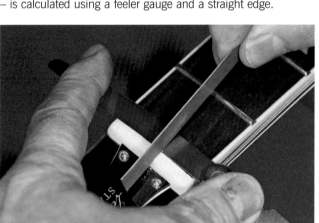

11 Secure the new nut in place with a couple of dabs of glue. Don't overdo the glue, as the nut may need removing again for correction.

12 Check the action at the 1st fret. A feeler gauge at the nut should register approximately .038in but this will naturally depend on the specific fret heights. This figure is arrived at by taking a measurement between the 1st and 2nd frets as shown and adding approx .005in for clearance and also subsequent nut wear.

File at a back angle, to shape the floor, or bottom, of the slot correctly, this enables the string to slide through freely. If the slot isn't correctly shaped, it will prevent smooth tuning and will hamper the instrument's ability to return to tune, particularly after using a vibrato.

When a string binds in the nut slot, it makes a pinging sound as it breaks free. This ping is often attributed to the tremolo/vibrato, as it's the use of the device that triggers the release of the snagging. The nut will eventually need lubricating with graphite (see box out). The back angle of the slot will give good contact for the string, important for tone, whilst a first contact point at the front (fret end) of the nut will ensure correct intonation. Ideally the bottom of the nut slot should be rounded as per the relevant string radius.

✎ Tech Tip

Graphite dust used for lock lubrication makes a good nut lubricant but it does tend to go everywhere when applied using the blower provided. Mixing a little graphite with some Vaseline petroleum jelly makes a useful and controllable lubricant paste. Apply it sparingly.

John Diggins – Luthier

Setting up an 'S' type vibrato

If your guitar is an 'S' type with a vibrato then setting this up correctly is vital. The alignment affects the overall string-height and so needs to be addressed before setting the saddles and the intonation.

Many 'S'-type guitars have a version of Leo Fender's 1954 vibrato. The detail varies, but the principles remain much the same. The only major change is the shift to a two-screw pivot rather than six. I recommend using a two-screw pivot set-up even on 'vintage-type' guitars, as the lower friction tends to better stability – you'll find the details below.

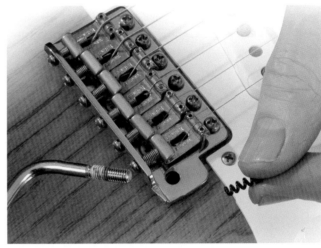

NB: To get started on a first guitar you could initially assume that the fulcrum 'bevel' is correct and try a basic set-up – so go on to 'Start here' section on page 50. However, if the set-up as supplied fails to return to pitch satisfactorily you may then want to tackle the critical bevel alignment or refer it to an expert.

The alignment described here applies to the vintage-style 'synchronised' tremolo. There are other 'S'-type and retro-fit vibratos available. For information on these see below.

■ Check the bevel

Leo Fender designed his tremolo on a very simple 'knife-edge' principle, which he first observed working effectively on a set of kitchen 'balance' weighing scales. This was exactly the principle he required, and depended on the strings providing one weight on the 'balance' and his tremolo springs the other. To work correctly this relies on a 'virtual' knife-edge between the bridge fixing screws and a countersunk hole in the bottom of the bridge plate.

It's worth checking for the correct bevel on the pivot points underneath the bridge. These could be worn or, more rarely, have never been quite right since manufacture.

Checking and lubricating the bevel

1 Remove the guitar strings – I recommend doing this one string at a time and working from the sixth and first inwards towards the fourth and third. This method prevents damage and misalignment caused by too much sudden stress and change in the neck tension.

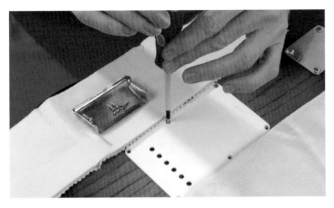

2 Using a No '1' Phillips screwdriver, carefully remove the plastic access cover located on the back of the guitar. Use a small plastic tray or paint-can lid to store the temporarily removed screws.

3 Unclip the tremolo springs – this may require a small set of pliers. Make a note of the spring order and arrangement (straight in this case, but sometimes trapezoid).

4 Unscrew the six bridge retaining screws with a No '2' Phillips screwdriver.

5 Examine the under bridge countersink. The rim should be between 3/64in and 1/16in thick and should be consistent for all six screws. If you decide to adjust the bevel you'll require a 'No 4' metalworkers' countersink. Do not contemplate this unless you're a skilled metalworker, as precision is required.

6 Lubricate the bevel with a little Vaseline or ChapStick.

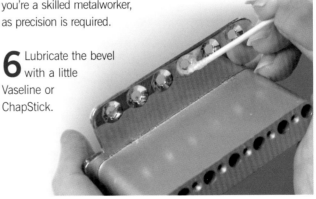

7 Reassemble, including replacing the trem springs.
NB: When replacing the bridge retaining screws follow the instructions given in steps 4 and 5 below. The tremolo springs must be back in place in order to set the bridge screw heights.
Restring the guitar but leave the tremolo rear access plate off for now.

■ Alignment Procedure

The Fender 'floating tremolo' design relies on establishing a balance between a consistent string tension and the set tension of the vibrato spring mechanism. If this balance is incorrect the vibrato will not function correctly; it will also be difficult to string the guitar via the rear access holes, as they're likely to be misaligned. In fact many Vintage Strats are missing the rear vibrato cover due to frustration over this issue.

For tremolo alignment with bevel already set

■ START HERE

1 Using a '1' point Phillips screwdriver carefully remove the plastic access cover located on the back of the guitar. Use a small plastic lid or Fender ashtray to store the screws. Remove the guitar strings.

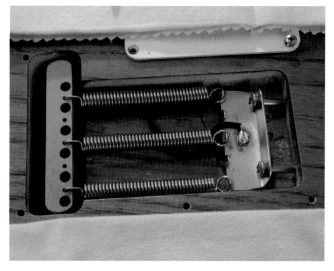

As so often happens Eric Clapton has permanently removed the rear access plate on 'Blackie'. Note also the blocked off trem and five springs.

2 Using a No '1' Phillips screwdriver loosen all six screws located at the front edge of the bridge plate. Raise them so that all of the screws measure approximately 1/16in (1.6mm) above the top of the bridge plate.

3 Now tighten the two outside screws until they're flush with the top of the bridge plate. Then loosen these two screws a quarter-turn. The bridge will pivot on the outside screws, leaving the four inside screws in place for bridge stability.

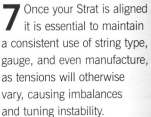

6 **Note** that you'll need to retune as required to get the right balance between the strings and the springs.

■ If you prefer a flush bridge to the body, adjust the spring tension to equal the string tension whilst the bridge rests on the body (you may want to add an extra half-turn to each claw screw to ensure that the bridge remains flush to the body during string bends).

CAUTION: Do not over-tighten these springs, as this can put unnecessary tension on the arm during tremolo use.

7 Once your Strat is aligned it is essential to maintain a consistent use of string type, gauge, and even manufacture, as tensions will otherwise vary, causing imbalances and tuning instability.

8 Replace rear cover using No '1' Phillips as before. Take care not to over-tighten the screws, as the thin plastic will tend to crack at the edges.

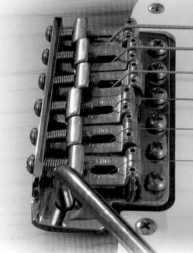

4 Restring the guitar and check your guitar is at either (a) standard pitch or (b) a custom pitch that you're opting to use consistently with this particular guitar. Use an electronic tuner set to your favoured pitch.

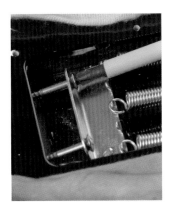

5 Ensuring that the bridge can float freely (no obstruction of the tremolo arm), use a No '2' Phillips screwdriver to adjust the 'claw' screws in the tremolo cavity.

■ Adjust the bridge to your desired angle (Fender factory specification is a 1/8in/3.2mm gap at the rear of the bridge, which is a good starting point).

✏ Tech Tip

Generally if the pivot is correctly engineered – and sometimes it does require a little subtle re-filing and sometimes 'centring' – then no lubrication is necessary. If you're having severe tuning problems take the guitar to an expert.

John Diggins – Luthier

Restringing a Floyd Rose vibrato

Some 'S' types and other solid guitars are equipped with Floyd Rose vibratos, which require a unique approach to stringing.

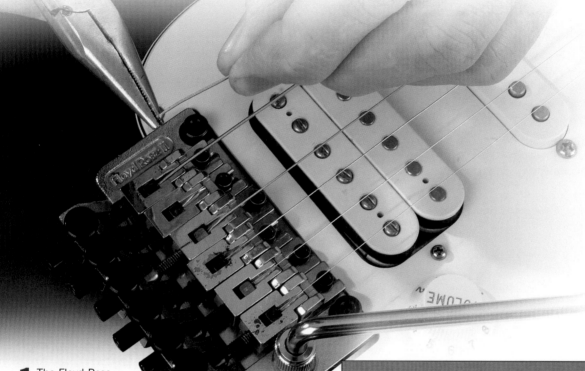

1 The Floyd Rose recommendation is to use DynaMaxx FR-End strings, which have no ball ends. However, if you prefer your own brand you need to start by cutting off the ball ends with a pair of substantial wire cutters – I favour the Draper expert long-handled type as they take a lot of wear and have plenty of torque, but cheaper, smaller ones will do the job for a short while. Make a careful note of the ball end colour code for the string gauges if this information is given on the packet.

■ Before cutting any wound string always make a 90° degree bend in the windings to avoid any unwinding.

2 Set the fine-tuners to their central position to give plenty of scope for adjustment.

Beware

Do not try this on a dark stage! If you're committed to gigging with a Floyd Rose, carry a spare guitar and preferably a guitar tech. It's easy to lose some of the smaller parts of the Floyd Rose saddle clamps during a string change.

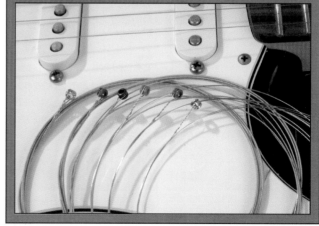

3 The old strings are removed by first de-tensioning the locking nut fasteners with a 3mm hex/Allen key. Then de-tension the strings via the machine heads as normal – Floyd Rose recommend replacing one string at a time to avoid unbalancing the trem. This is good practice on any guitar.

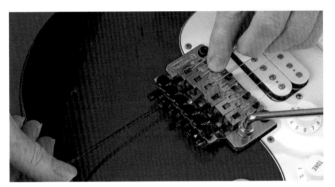

4 De-tension the individual hex/Allen fastener at the saddle end. I recommend a long shank 3mm key for this, as it usually requires a lot of torque. Also the long shank just clears the body, avoiding any paintwork damage – though you should take the usual precaution of positioning a rag or duster behind the saddles.

Remove the old string and de-thread it from the locking nut. The bare end of the new string can then be positioned in the block and the Allen key clamp re-tensioned. Do not over-tension, as this may damage the thread.

5 Thread the new string through the loosened locking nut and affix as normal to the machine head. Repeat for all six strings, working in from the sixth and first strings, thus maintaining an even tension on the neck. Always put a string on under tension.

6 Tune the guitar to pitch and thoroughly stretch the strings.

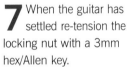

7 When the guitar has settled re-tension the locking nut with a 3mm hex/Allen key.

8 Recheck the tuning, this time using the fine-tuners.

The Paul Bigsby vibrato

Designed by Paul Adelburt Bigsby (1899–1968), and currently made in Savannah, Georgia, USA (as well as being licensed for Far Eastern copies), the Bigsby guitar vibrato arm is another classic vibrato often found on 'T' types, 'LP' types and every Rockabilly guitar. It is probably the second most famous vibrato after Leo Fender's 'synchronised floating trem'.

In the late 1940s Paul Bigsby, Les Paul and Leo Fender were all friends and together they kicked around ideas for a solid-bodied guitar with the then fashionable vibrato-glissandi and rich sustain qualities of an 'Hawaiian' steel guitar. They all came up with slightly different solutions to this challenge and Paul Bigsby was certainly in the vibrato arm business before Leo (probably as early as 1948, while Leo's appearing in 1954).

In truth the Bigsby arm is not as innovative as Leo's and is both very heavy and perhaps a little clumsier in operation. However, it does have its own distinctive character of vibrato, heard to great effect on the recordings of Duane Eddy, Chet Atkins and many Rockabilly guitarists.

Strangely the Bigsby is most associated with hollow body Gretsch and Gibson models, not solid body guitars. However, the Les Paul guitar became available with a Bigsby to special order from the early 1950s, and several high profile guitarists – including Les Paul, Mick Taylor and Keith Richards – have used Bigsby appointed Les Pauls.

Practicalities and intonation issues

Perhaps the first thing to consider with a Bigsby is weight! Les Paul 'Black Beauties' weigh 9½lb (4.3kg) without a trem and 10½lb (4.8kg) with. This is an aluminium trem with gold plating – the B7G model, with custom black infilling on the Bigsby logo and a gap in the heel plate for a strap fixing.

Although the Bigsby is less subtle and responsive than Leo Fender's or any of the other 'synchronised' trems, there *are* plus factors with Paul Bigsby's design.

■ The extra weight behind the Tune-O-Matic bridge does give more rigidity and 'tone' to the guitar's acoustic and amplified sound, perhaps lowering the guitar's principal resonant frequency – often a beneficial effect.

■ Unlike a 'floating' vibrato, the single powerful 'motorcycle compression' spring of the Bigsby causes much less pitch discrepancy when physically bending strings, *ie* you can manually pitch bend strings one, two and three whilst sustaining a pedal bass note, and the latter remains *relatively* stable. Try this on a floating Strat trem and you may unintentionally enter the world of bitonality!

■ By the same token a broken string on a correctly set up Bigsby guitar will leave the rest of the guitar fairly in tune. On a floating trem you enter the world of atonality.

However, keeping a Bigsby working well and even replacing strings does set certain unique challenges.

The first thing to know is that there are at least 12 different variants of the Bigsby vibrato, some cosmetic but many critical to its effective use. If you have an LP with a factory-fitted Bigsby it will be the correct type. However, retro-fitted Bigsbys need to be carefully selected and Bigsby currently offer aluminium and 'gold'-plated types specifically with the LP in mind. These are the B7, B70 and B12, all offered in plain aluminium or 'gold' plated. Other Bigsby units are available for most guitar types.

Maintenance

■ Lubricate the spring extremely sparingly – over-lubrication may cause damage to the all-important 'cushion' washer.

■ Lubricate the whole string path – the nut with graphite, saddles with a microscopic amount of '3 in 1' oil and the Bigsby roller with a little Vaseline or ChapStick. Be especially careful not to stain any 'gold'-plated fittings where present.

■ Replacement springs, fibre washers and bearings are readily available from Bigsby, and a 50-year-old trem may often benefit from replacement of these heavily mechanical parts – any wear-induced discrepancies will naturally affect the precarious stability of the mechanism.

■ For tuning stability it's essential to ensure that all the fitting screws are tight. This requires a No '2' Phillips for the top fixings and a No '1' for the end plate.

Stringing a Bigsby-fitted guitar

1 Crimp the new string into a curve at the ball end – an awkward job!

2 Feed the string underneath, around and over the axle.

3 Place the ball end of the string on to the axle pin.

4 Keep the tension on the string with a capo at the 7th fret holding the ball in place on the axle.

5 You could alternatively try pushing a wedge of foam rubber into the space under the axle to keep the string in place on the pin during winding.

6 Wind the string on to the tuning machine, tune to pitch, remove the capo and/or the foam wedge.

String trees – 'S' and 'T' types

Having sorted out any vibrato issues, be sure to check the string tree next – for guitar tuning stability, it's the little things that count. The humble string tree is not the most glamorous aspect of a guitar, but if it's awry the guitar is doomed to be constantly out of tune – and usually it's the vibrato or the tuning heads that get the blame! When setting up a new guitar always lubricate the string tree and the nut with a little graphite from a pencil tip and/or Lubrikit.

'String guide' variants

From their very inception the Fender 'S'-type and 'T'-type guitars were different. Virtually every other guitar ever made up until 1948 had a headstock that angled back away from the nut. This convention ensured downward pressure on the nut, which both keeps the strings in place and ensured a good tone.

Leo Fender was different. His 'working man's' guitar would be lean, mean and efficient. Curiously his innovation saves wood, which is good for productivity and also for the environment. Having saved some wood and created a distinctive and very different headstock (based, he says, on some Croatian guitars he'd seen*), Leo was left with a problem – too little break-angle at the nut – which he solved for the 'Broadcaster' guitar in 1950 by introducing a round string guide to pull the first and second strings in towards the neck. This round string guide is still found on some very early Strats but is more often replaced by a custom-made 'string tree', which does the same job.

■ The slightest touch of lubrication here (using Lipsalve, ChapStick or Vaseline) will avoid any 'sticking' causing intonation problems. This particularly applies when heavy use is made of the vibrato/tremolo arm.

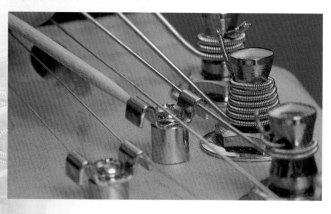

* The Croatian guitars still used in Istria have this distinctive Stauffer type of headstock, but I'm not sure of how Stauffer links with Istria, though I suspect the link is Istria's cultural links with Venice.

■ The adoption by many guitarists of a plain unwound third string may have been the prompt for Fender to adopt a second string tree in the early '70s. This covers the third and fourth string and is aesthetically a neater solution than a single or triple 'tree'.

American Series 2000 onwards

A third option found on the 'American Series' Strats which replaced the American Standard in 2000, features a neat combination of a low friction 'roller'-type string tree for the first and second strings combined with staggered lower string posts for the top four strings. This is an effective solution to the 'nut tension' issue.

Exceptions

The string tree would only be an encumbrance on any of the 'Superstrats' that incorporate roller bridges, such as 2002's Fender American Deluxe Fat Strat or Richie Sambora's locking trem Signature guitar. Naturally the locking bar of a Floyd Rose ensures plenty of downward pressure at the nut seen below. Some late model 'S' types have staggered tuner pegs to assist with correct nut angle issues – and so the evolution continues.

Very occasionally string trees may have been positioned incorrectly at the factory. This means that the desirable 'straight pull' which Leo intended is distorted. Remedying this without leaving unsightly holes in the headstock is a job for a well-equipped and skilled luthier.

> ### 🖊 Tech Tip
>
> **The extra string tree helps when an inexperienced player replacing his strings doesn't allow enough windings on the string post, leaving a fairly gentle slope up to the nut – the string spacer provides the necessary pressure at the nut.**
>
> ***Andy Gibson of London's Tin Pan Alley***

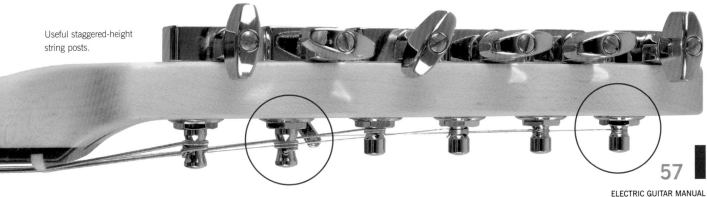

Useful staggered-height string posts.

Bridge height and intonation – 'S' & 'T' types

NB: If your guitar is without a Fender, Wilkinson or Floyd Rose-type 'floating' vibrato then you can set the bridge height and intonation straight after setting the truss rod and the nut.

Part 1: Setting the string height

One of the joys of modern bridge design is the ability to adjust individual string heights as well as effective string length.

■ So why might you want to adjust individual string height?
The most likely reason is to correctly reflect the radius of the fingerboard, or perhaps you're just curious. Leo Fender would approve – he built his whole guitar concept around satisfying individual player's requirements. This built-in versatility has resulted in one genius design being used happily by players as diverse as Hank Marvin, Jimmy Hendrix and Joe Walsh. More likely you're trying to achieve a lower, more playable action.

If you're playing bottleneck guitar you may need to set the strings quite high to avoid catching the frets with your slide.

If you're playing slinky blues with a light picking style you may find a very 'low' action workable.

1950s innovation

As a working engineer Leo Fender would have been aware that the Gretsch company had introduced individual string length adjustment in 1952 with the six-saddle 'Melita Synchro-sonic' bridge designed by Sebastiano (Johnny) Melita, and Gibson had introduced their 'Tunomatic' bridge circa 1953.

String height parameters eventually come down to personal taste and your individual sound. However, Fender do offer some recommendations for 'average' set-ups:

Neck radius	String height bass side	String height treble side
7.25in	5⁄64in/.0781in	4⁄64in/1⁄16in/.0625in
9.5in to 12in	4⁄64in	4⁄64in
15in to 17in	4⁄64in	3⁄64in/.0469in

For details of your guitar's neck radius refer to the specific case studies in this book or use a radius gauge.

Tech Tip

Should you lose one of the screws the threads on the Fender vintage saddle's tiny grub screws are 4-40 UNC.

John Diggins – Luthier

1 Check the current action height at the 17th fret with a car feeler gauge. In practice this means either combining several individual feeler gauges to make up 1/16in or the decimal equivalent value of .0625in; or, using a 6in ruler (with 1/32in and 1/64in increments), measuring the distance between the bottom of the strings and the top of the 17th fret.

2 With, usually, a .05in Allen key, use the two pivot adjustment screws to achieve the desired overall string height for the first string at the 17th fret. Vintage guide height is 4/64in (1/16in/.0625in) on the classic 7.25in radius.

Tech Tip

I find it best to set the first string height first, as this is often the most critical on an 'S' or 'T' type. Set the first string high enough to avoid 'choking' when bending the string in the high fret positions. The other string heights should then follow the neck radius pattern.

John Diggins – Luthier

3 Adjust the sixth string bridge saddle to height according to the above chart recommendations, then adjust the other bridge saddles to follow the neck radius as indicated by the appropriate under-string radius gauge. Retune the guitar. **NB:** For propriety radius gauges please see the *Useful contacts* appendix.

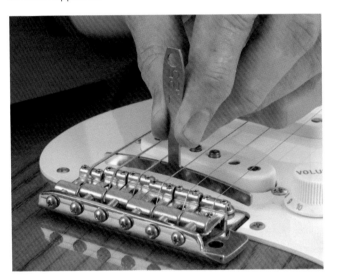

These recommended action settings and radius measurements are, of course, only a guide. You can obviously experiment with the individual saddle height until your desired sound and feel is achieved.

Note that adjusting string heights affects the effective sounding length of the string, and this naturally affects intonation, so you will now need to refer to Part 2 of this chapter, 'Setting the working string length'.

It is also important to note that the magnetic field of the conventional 'S' and 'T'-type pickup can be strong enough to interfere with the string's normal excursion, and this can have further implications for accurate intonation – see page 86 for more on this.

Part 2: Setting the working string length

Leo Fender's original design incorporated the ability to adjust individual string lengths.

■ So why would you want to do this?

If the guitar has not been maintained for some years, or if you've recently changed your string gauges, you may notice that as you ascend the fingerboard in normal playing, the guitar is not sounding 'in tune'.

A little background

There are two basic ways of changing the pitch of a vibrating guitar string – you can increase or decrease the string tension by adjusting the machine heads, as in normal tuning, or you can alter the string length by normal fretting on the fingerboard.

The frets on the fingerboard are arranged in a mathematical series of ascending decreasing intervals. The frets get closer together as we ascend to what guitarist Martin Taylor refers to as 'the dusty end of the fingerboard'. We won't get bogged down in the maths here, but you could perhaps impress the drummer by dropping the phrases 'rule of 18' or 'Pythagorean equation' into pre-gig drinks conversation. Look it up – it may inspire a new song.

The assumption of the correct function of the carefully worked out fret intervals is that the string itself has a defined length. If all your guitar's strings were the same gauge or thickness we could dispense with Leo's invention and simply have a 'straight line' arrangement of the bridge saddles.

In the real world your first string could be .009 gauge and your sixth string .042. The four other strings are usually gauged somewhere between these two. Fretting a string changes its tension slightly. A difference in string diameter affects the amount of change in string tension as it is fretted. This means that to sound 'in tune' the first string benefits from having a shorter effective length than the second string and so on. Hence Leo's innovation.

- Take care to protect the guitar paintwork with a duster, taped in place with low-adhesion masking tape.

1 Tune the open string to E concert. Check the harmonic note at the 12th fret of the first string as compared to the same fretted note (clearly the harmonic note contains less of the 'fundamental' pitch note than the fretted note; this should not affect the adjustment). All the sounded notes should be precisely the same pitch though in different octaves. A practised ear will detect any discrepancy. An alternative solution is to use an extremely accurate electronic tuner, which will visually display any discrepancy in 'cents', either 'flat' or 'sharp'.

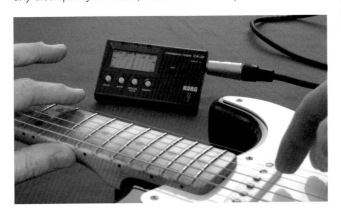

2 If the string sounds or indicates 'flat' at the 12th fret when compared with the 12th harmonic, turn the longitudinal screw anticlockwise, thereby moving the saddle towards the neck.

If the note at the 12th fret sounds 'sharp' as compared to the harmonic then the string length is too short and the saddle should be adjusted clockwise.

Adjust until the harmonic, open string and 12th fret all indicate or sound at the same pitch. Repeat this procedure for all six strings.

Note that raising or lowering the string saddles as in Part 1 of this chapter, *Setting the string height*, will effectively alter the string length, so essentially these two operations should be considered together.

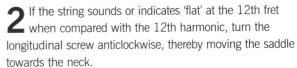

Tech Tip

It's worth checking the intonation at the 19th fret of the first string (B natural) against the open B string. If the open B and E are in tune then the 19th fret and open B should not 'beat'. This applies equally to the 20th fret on the B string and the open G string. Similar checks should be tried on the 19th fret for all other strings.

John Diggins – Luthier

Neck adjustment – all bolt-on necks

Due to the 'handmade', pre-computer nature of the manufacture of many early 'T' and 'S' types there may often be a slight variance in neck pitch in relation to the body. This can have critical implications for perceived action, string height and the setting of the bridge saddles. Correcting this in practice means placing a wooden shim approximately .01in (0.25 mm) thick in the neck pocket, underneath the butt of the neck.

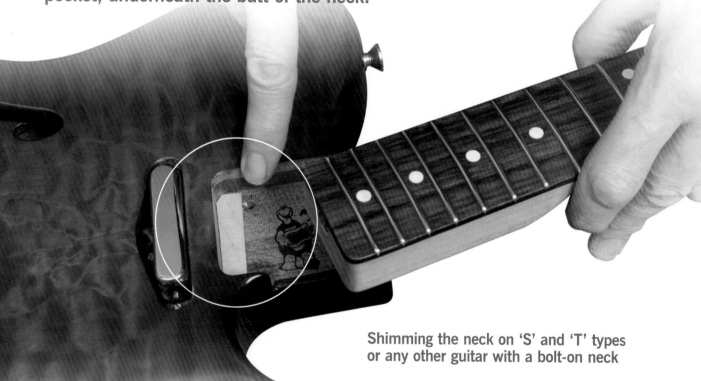

Tech Tip

If you cannot achieve a workable action with the bridge grub screws set at their lowest then you probably need a shim in the neck cavity.

John Diggins – Luthier

Shimming the neck on 'S' and 'T' types or any other guitar with a bolt-on neck

■ **Why would you want to do this?**

The need to adjust the pitch of the neck occurs in situations where the string height is high and the action adjustment is as low as the saddle adjustment will allow.

'Shimming' is the time-honoured procedure used to adjust the pitch of a bolt-on neck. But note that the pitch of the neck on your guitar should have been preset at the factory and in most cases will not need to be adjusted. However, old 'S' and 'T' types have often been repaired/adjusted and 'shims' are often lost or removed accidentally.

Micro-Tilt adjustment

On many of the Fender American series 'S' and 'T'-type guitars, Micro-Tilt adjustment is offered. This uses an Allen key adjustment working against a plate installed in the butt-end of the neck. The need to adjust the pitch of the neck (raising the butt-end of the neck in the pocket, thereby pitching the neck back) occurs in situations where the string height is high and the action adjustment is as low as the bridge adjustment will allow.

For those guitars with Micro-Tilt adjustment, loosen the two neck screws on both sides of the adjustment access hole on the neckplate by at least four full turns. Tightening the hex adjustment screw with a 1/8in hex wrench by approximately a quarter-turn will allow you to raise the action approximately 1/32in. Retighten the neck screws when the adjustment is complete.

1 Remove the strings. I suggest removing the strings one at a time – sixth, then first, then fifth and second. This spreads the tension loss evenly as opposed to removing all the strings at once, as a sudden change of tension can impose tremendous shock to the timber of the neck, with potential for distortion.

2 Unscrew the four neck screws using a No '2' Phillips screwdriver.

3 Remove the neck gently from its seating in the pocket of the body. Note carefully the position of any existing shims if present.

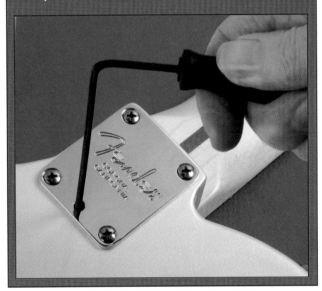

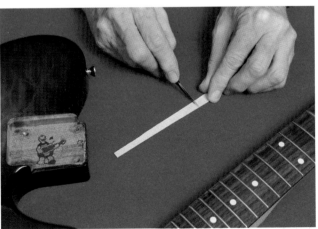

4 A new shim approximately ¼in (6.4mm) wide x 1¾in (44.5mm) long x .01in (0.25mm) thick will allow you to raise the action by about 1/32in (0.8 mm).

5 Ease the new shim into position and carefully maintain its position whilst replacing the neck in its slot. Replace the neck fixing screws.

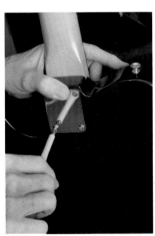

String height and intonation on a Tune-O-Matic

Though a Gibson innovation this type of bridge is now common to many 'LP', 'SG' and 'Archtop' guitars.

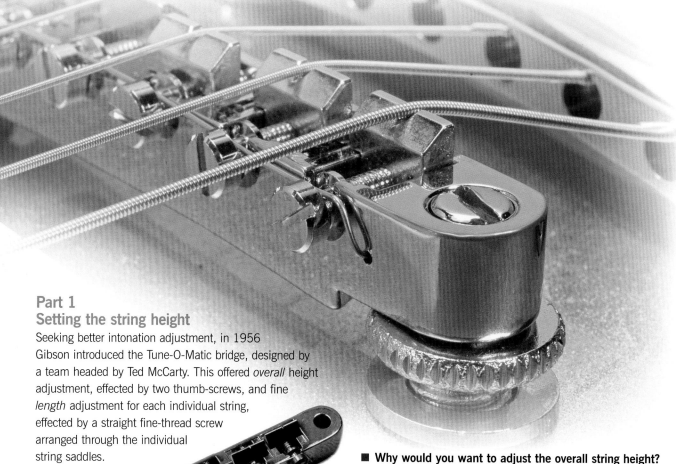

Part 1
Setting the string height

Seeking better intonation adjustment, in 1956 Gibson introduced the Tune-O-Matic bridge, designed by a team headed by Ted McCarty. This offered *overall* height adjustment, effected by two thumb-screws, and fine *length* adjustment for each individual string, effected by a straight fine-thread screw arranged through the individual string saddles.

More recent budget-line Epiphone Tune-O-Matics have a 'top screw' arrangement which makes height adjustment easier (see page 65).

■ **Why would you want to adjust the overall string height?**
Perhaps you're experimenting with different string gauges to achieve a different sound or style of playing – heavy gauge strings ideal for bottleneck slide guitar or super slinky 009s for three-semitone string bends? These extremes will require significant bridge adjustment.

String heights and all their parameters eventually come down to the preferences and styles of individual players. However, here are the Gibson recommended working references for an average 'LP' set-up:

Neck radius	String height at the 12th fret	
12in	Bass side	Treble side
	5/64in	3/64in

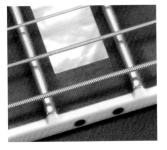

1 Check the current action height at the 12th fret with a regular car feeler gauge. This will probably entail the combining of several individual gauges to make up the guideline recommendation of 3/64in on the treble side.

An alternative approach would be to use a metalworkers' steel rule with the required 1/32 and 1/64 increments (or decimal equivalent). The critical measurement is the distance from the top of the fret to the bottom of the string.

2 If the action measures too high on the treble side then turning the Tune-O-Matic thumbscrew clockwise will lower the action. Do this slowly, checking all the time for any severe 'fret buzz' resulting from going too low, until the desired compromise is reached. Bear
in mind that the simple two-point engineering involved will mean that to some extent all the strings will be lowered.

The same operation can be achieved on some Tune-O-Matics with a 5.5mm flathead screwdriver in the top slot – this adjustment option is most commonly found on Epiphone guitars. Again a clockwise micro-turn takes the bridge down (shown for bass strings). **NB:** The bridge responds quickly, so make any turns in small increments.

3 Make a similar measurement and adjustment to the bass side of the bridge and recheck any effects on the treble.

Obviously a 'too low' bridge can equally be corrected by an anticlockwise adjustment of the thumb-screws.

Raising a Tune-O-Matic is sometimes difficult, as you're working against the downward pressure of the strings. The answer is to use a 'Tune-O-Medic' bridge jack – not forcing the thumb-screws with a pair of finish-endangering pliers!

Often the crude two-point adjustment can still leave some individual strings too high or too low. This is best checked with a radius gauge.

4 If an individual saddle is too high then carefully and slowly filing the slot with a gauged nut file will do the trick – always checking constantly with the radius gauge. **NB:** Always file to leave the fulcrum edge at the 'neck' side of the saddle, at the same time avoiding filing the 'body' of the bridge!

5 If an individual saddle is too low then the choice is between lowering all the others to match, and then raising the whole bridge, *or* fitting a new individual saddle. This choice must obviously be made on the basis of the severity of the specific misalignment. The saddles are available 'un-notched' from the usual outlets (see *Useful contacts* appendix).

Bear in mind that the lowering or raising of the bridge will necessarily affect the effective sounding length of the string, and this will inevitably require adjustment of the Tune-O-Matic's individual saddle screws to achieve a precise octave at the 12th fret – see below.

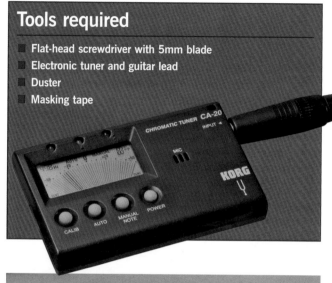
Part 2
Intonation – setting the working string lengths

The Tune-O-Matic enables precise setting of the individual string lengths to achieve a perfect octave at the 12th fret.

■ Why would you need to do this?

If you change the Tune-O-Matic height, the gauge of your strings or adjust the truss rod it's likely that the precise individual string lengths will have also changed. The result is that when fretted your guitar sounds out of tune even when the open strings seem precisely 'in-tune'.

I recommend you find a gauge of string that works for you, set the guitar up, and stick with that gauge.

■ Intonation

The fine setting of the intonation should be attempted only *after* a comfortable bridge height has been established (see page 65).

1 Tune the open first string to E concert 440Hz. Check the 12th fret stopped note – is it the same? An electronic guitar tuner is a useful aid to a precise scientific assessment. This will display any discrepancy in cents, either sharp or flat. Both these notes and the 'octave' (12th fret) harmonic should be the same.

Tune-O-Matics can be fitted with screw heads facing the tailpiece *or* facing the pickups (the original arrangement); the guidance offered here refers to the latter. If your guitar has the former arrangement then the clockwise/anticlockwise instructions will necessarily reverse!

Note that a little masking tape or a well-placed duster on the pickup cover or stop bar will avoid accidental scratches caused by the screwdriver.

2 If the string sound indicates flat at the 12th fret when compared to the 12th harmonic turn the saddle length adjustment screw clockwise, thereby moving the saddle towards the neck (shortening the effective sounding length).

If the note at the 12th fret sounds sharp when compared to the harmonic then the sounding length is too short, and the saddle screw should be adjusted anticlockwise.

Adjust until the harmonic, 12th fret and open string all indicate the same note. Repeat the process for all six strings.

Sometimes when you run out of 'travel' and the note is still flat or sharp at the 12th fret, the Tune-O-Matic saddles have to be reversed. This is a simple enough procedure, only occasionally made difficult by the saddle retaining spring.

This can be awkward to remove – a little persuasion with some fine-nosed pliers and a suitably taped-up screwdriver usually does the trick, but *go gently*, as you need the spring to retain its shape to remain effective when reinstalled.

Sometimes on reversal the saddle notch will need re-filing, ensuring the fulcrum edge is at the pickup side of the saddle.

Replacing the spring is another 'go gently' operation using suitably protected fine-nose pliers.

✎ Tech Tip

NB: This also applies to 'LP's. It's worth checking the intonation at the 19th fret of the first string (B natural) against the open B string. If the open B and E are in tune then the 19th fret and open B should not 'beat'. This applies equally to the 20th fret on the B string and the open G string. Similar checks should be tried on the 19th fret for all other strings.

John Diggins – Luthier

Do-it-yourself 'hard tail'

If you don't need a vibrato you may find a hard tail conversion stabilises your 'S'-type's tuning

When Leo and his colleagues designed the Stratocaster they were improving what they called 'The Fender guitar', and the addition of a vibrato/tremolo mechanism took them nearer to their ideal of a guitar that sounded closer to a steel or Hawaiian guitar. This would better serve their 'Western Swing' customers. It also worked brilliantly for instrumental bands such as The Ventures in the USA and The Shadows in the UK, who quickly developed a whole new technique built on the creative use of the 'Vibrato'.

Their guitars, like every other guitar of that era, were strung with medium or heavy gauge strings, and the use of string 'bending' techniques to achieve a portamento effect was not only rare but also – with such heavy strings – difficult.

The development of urban blues in Chicago in the '50s and '60s found Buddy Guy and his contemporaries experimenting with the new Fender guitars and stringing them with much lighter strings to better facilitate 'string bending' for portamento effects. It's thought this may have been seen as an alternative to using the 'bottleneck' technique common in acoustic country blues.

As light gauge strings were not yet commercially available, players often substituted a light gauge banjo G string for the E first string and used the E string as a second string. The B string became the first unwound 'plain' third, replacing the then normal wound third,

which became the new fourth, and so on. Country music players in Nashville adopted the same modification and for a period the string substitution was commonly referred to as 'Nashville stringing'.

When you use string bending techniques with a standard Fender 'synchronised tremolo'/vibrato there is a natural tendency for the whole 'floating bridge' assembly to move, effectively cancelling some of the string bending effect and also detuning all the other 'unbent' strings. Though this didn't bother Jimi Hendrix or Jeff Beck, who both utilised the effect as part of their style, it doesn't appeal to everyone.

Several players devised homemade solutions to this issue. Screwing the bridge hard down to the body is one of them, and blocking the tremolo string block with a piece of wood is another.

Fender realised some players wanted a 'hard tail' version of the Strat and offered one as an ex-factory item as early as April 1955. However, this option has never proved very popular. It would seem quite logical that the metal of the trem block and even the trem springs must contribute something to the distinctive Strat sound. For example, the Eric Clapton Signature model has a blocked-off trem, though Eric never uses it, so he clearly feels the mechanism is worth retaining for its secondary tonal effect.

A Practical Approach

1 Remove the strings one at a time, working from the outer two inwards – *ie* first and sixth, then second and fifth, then third and fourth. This will avoid putting the guitar neck through any sudden changes in tension and will mean less resetting.

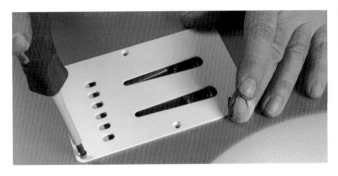

2 Carefully remove the plastic backplate from the tremolo/vibrato cavity using a Phillips No '1' screwdriver.

3 Check which kind of trem block is fitted to your guitar – this could be a classic '50s- and '60s-style solid steel block or a much lighter and tapered cast alloy block as found on Squiers and many copies.

4 Carefully measure the cavity – a digital vernier gauge is ideal for this.

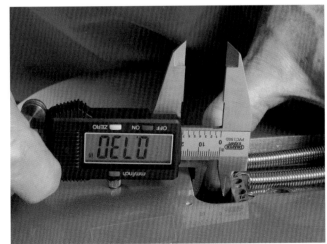

5 From a small scrap of hardwood, fashion a custom block to fit the tapers inside the cavity behind the existing metal tremolo block. This will be approximately 0.5in/12mm thick by 3in/7.5cm long by as much as 1.75in/4cm deep, though you should rough-cut it slightly oversize and custom sand it for a snug fit. The John Diggins example illustrated is actually quite small but effective.

6 With the trem springs as a grip, the new hardwood block should hold itself snugly in position.

NB: At least one of the trem springs should be left in place, as this provides earth or ground continuity via the wiring to the spring 'claw'. As they contribute to the sound they're best all left in place – Eric Clapton has five in the back of his 'hard tail' Strat.

7 Replace the plastic tremolo cover plate. You may want to consider replacing the cover with the latest Fender American Series type. This has larger access holes for stringing and the metal vibrato block may now be otherwise difficult to access in its new blocked-off position.

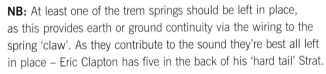

Improving your guitar's performance

The electric guitar is a fairly delicate mechanical instrument that performs at its best in response to a little maintenance. This includes keeping an eye out for developing problems like fret wear as well as doing a little simple lubrication of moving parts and friction points. As the electrics inevitably wear out – pots and switches are prone to electrical crackles, and even going 'open circuit' – replacement with higher-grade components is money well spent. Economy guitars are also often supplied with cheap low-grade pickups and upgrading them is the most obvious and relatively simple way of effectively improving the sound of your instrument.

LEFT 'Aged' Squier pickup covers.

RIGHT An Epiphone Les Paul 'Plus' top.

Safety first

Generally speaking the electric guitar is no more dangerous to play or work on than its acoustic ancestor. However, there are some hazards of which you should be aware.

Electric shock

Sadly many players have either been killed or badly burned through accidental exposure to mains current. Though the UK's adoption of 240V may seem to present a greater risk than the USA's 110V, it's actually the amperes that are the killer, not the volts! Amperes are the measure of current, and high currents are the ones to avoid.

Guitar amplifiers run happily on domestic supplies at relatively low current ratings, so the situation of one guitarist one amp is a pretty safe scenario, especially if we observe a few precautions:

■ Always ensure a good earth or ground connection. This allows a safe path to earth for any stray current, which always flows along the easiest path. The earth or ground connection offers a quicker route to earth than through you and therein lies its safety potential.
■ Never replace fuses with the wrong value, eg a 5-amp fuse in a 3-amp socket. Fuses are there to protect us and our equipment from power surges. A higher value means less protection. Never replace a fuse with a bodge such as silver foil or similar. This offers no protection at all.
■ Consider using an earth leakage trip or similar circuit-breaker in any situation where you have no control of the mains power.
■ Maintain your mains leads. Check them regularly for damage and strained wires. If fitted the earth wire must be in place.
■ Never operate an amplifier with the safety cover removed, especially valve amplifiers known for their HT circuits.
■ Never put drinks on or near amplifiers.
■ Never touch a stage lighting circuit or lamp. Apart from mains electricity issues they're often also dangerously hot. Leave stage lamps to qualified electricians.

Beware of

■ Multi amp/multi PA scenarios that aren't professionally administered. Professional PA and lighting supervisors are very safety-conscious and trained in health and safety to a legal minimum requirement. The danger comes with 'semi pro' and amateur rigs which are not closely scrutinised. If you're in any doubt don't plug in until you've talked to the on-site supervisor and feel you can trust his assurances.

■ Unknown stage situations, especially those that feature big lighting rigs. This is easily said but hard to adhere to. Even the most modest gigs nowadays have quite sophisticated lights and sound. The crucial issue is that all the audio equipment is connected to the same PHASE. Danger particularly arises when microphones are connected to one PHASE and guitars and basses to another. A bass/vocalist could find himself as the 'bridge' between 30 amps of current! If in any doubt be rude and ask.

Hearing damage

Leo Fender's first guitar amp knocked out a feverish 4W of audio; but by the early '60s Paul McCartney had a T60. By 1964 The Beatles had the first 100W Vox amps, specifically made to cope with concerts in vast football stadiums and the noise of immense screaming crowds.

By 1970 100W was the norm for a guitar 'head' in a small club and the first 10,000W PA systems had rocked Woodstock.

Pete Townshend of The Who first complained of the hearing impairment tinnitus in the mid-'70s and for many years refused to tour with a band as his hearing worsened.

The key to saving your hearing is 'dose' figures. Research has shown that you risk damage if exposed to sound 'dose' levels of 90dB or above for extended periods. Health and safety limits for recording studios now recommend no more than 90dBA

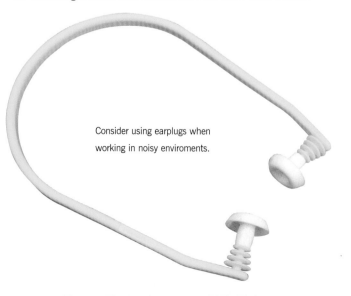

Consider using earplugs when working in noisy enviroments.

Chemical hazards

Paints and solvents

Traditionally electric guitars were painted with nitrocellulose lacquer and this practice continues on many, especially Vintage reissues. Nitrocellulose lacquers produce a very hard yet flexible, durable finish that can be polished to a high gloss. The drawbacks of these lacquers include the hazardous nature of the solvent, which is flammable, volatile and toxic. The dangers inherent in the inhalation of spray paints are serious enough to be covered by legal statutes in the USA, UK and Europe.

Masks can provide some protection against solvents and paint.

Symptoms
- **Acute and chronic ingestion:** Large doses may cause nausea, narcosis, weakness, drowsiness and unconsciousness.
- **Inhalation:** Irritation to nose and throat. At high concentrations, same effects as ingestion.
- **Skin:** Cracking of skin, dermatitis, and secondary infections.
- **Eyes:** Irritation.
- **Symptoms of overexposure:** Repeated skin contact may cause dermatitis, while the skin defatting properties of this material may aggravate an existing dermatitis. (Source: Material Safety Data Sheet.)

Polyurethane hazards

Vapours may accumulate in inadequately ventilated/confined areas, and may form explosive mixtures with air. Vapours may travel long distances and flashback may occur. Closed containers may explode when exposed to extreme heat.

Symptoms
- **Ingestion:** May be similar to inhalation symptoms – drowsiness, dizziness, nausea, irritation of digestive tract, depression, aspiration hazard.

- **Inhalation:** Dizziness, drowsiness, fatigue, weakness, headache, unconsciousness.
- **Skin:** Drying, cracking, dermatitis.
- **Eyes:** Burning, tearing, reddening. Possible transient corneal injury or swelling of conjunctiva. (Source: Carbon Black Carcinogen by IARC, Symptoms of Overexposure.)

Recommended precautions

Always wear goggles/full face shield and other protective equipment. Avoid skin contact by wearing protective clothing. Take a shower and bathe your eyes after exposure. Wash contaminated clothing thoroughly before reusing it. … So, with all this in mind, remember that the addresses of recommended guitar repair men and spray shops can be found in your local *Yellow Pages*.

If you really feel you want to customise your guitar then you must take extreme precautions, particularly to avoid inhalation of the dangerous mist created by the spray process.

A passive mask available from DIY stores will only offer the most minimal protection. If in any doubt consult the paint manufacturer for detailed precautions specific to the paint type you've chosen.

('A' standing for average) per eight-hour day, these levels to be reduced dramatically if the period is longer or the dBA higher.

Transient peaks, as in those produced by a loud snare drum or hi-hat, can easily push levels beyond these figures. Be careful where you stand in relation to drums and amplifiers – a small movement can effect a dramatic change in transient sound level. Don't be afraid to ask about peak and average

levels. Your ears are your greatest asset as a musician, so don't be embarrassed into thinking you can't question sound levels.

Repetitive strain injury

Guitarists need to think about posture, warm-up routines and avoiding over-practising. RSI is not funny and affects millions of players. Generate good habits early and stick to them.

Tools and working facilities

Many guitar adjustments can be done using regular domestic workshop tools, and a good working instrument should be easy to maintain. However, specialist luthier's tools can often make jobs easier and safer.

Necessary workshop tools

Many of the tools listed below can double up as your essential gig bag wrap, but as you don't have to carry all these tools around we can be less concerned about weight and portability. Consequently it's very convenient, for instance, to have separate screwdrivers rather than the interchangeable bit variety. Heftier wire cutters also make string changing a little easier.

■ Set of Phillips-type screwdrivers, sizes '0', '1' and '2'

It may seem a small point, but I recommend using the correct size and type of screwdriver. Many valuable guitars have survived 30 years on the road but often have a selection of odd screws and 'stripped' screw heads. These look unsightly, slow down maintenance and make the simplest job a chore. The correct 'point' size will reduce screw stripping and is also less likely to skate across your prized paintwork.

■ Use type '0' for some Kluson-type machine heads and truss rod shields.
■ Use type '1' for pickguard, rear access covers, jack socket, some machine-head screws and strap buttons.
■ Use type '2' for neck bolts.

A screwdriver with interchangeable heads is an alternative option. However, you'll often need several heads at the same time, which means a lot of changing around. This option is nevertheless useful on the road, when a compact toolkit is more practical.

Sometimes an electric screwdriver can take the strain out of repetitive tasks. However, be sure to protect the guitar as the screwdriver 'torques out'. Never use one on plastic parts, as old plastics become brittle and easily crack under sudden pressure.

The tools used in our case studies.

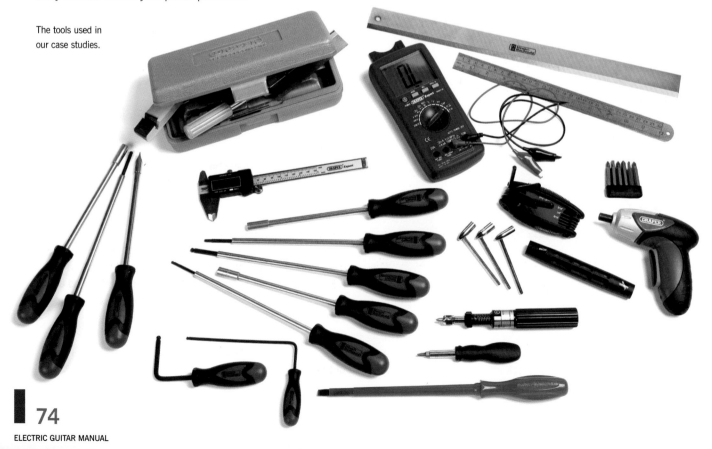

■ **Set of car feeler gauges (.002–.025in) (0.05–1mm)**
These are used for assessing and setting the string action height.

■ **12in (150 mm) ruler with 1/32in and 1/64in increments (0.5mm increments)**
Used for setting and assessing the string action.

■ **Light machine oil (3-in-1 or equivalent)**
Can be used sparingly for lubricating the string path.

■ **4mm straight-slot screwdriver**
For early Fenders.

■ **Large straight slot screwdriver**
For some truss rods.

■ **Portable suction fixing vice**
This ingenious device is terrific if you have no suitable permanent workbench. Ideal for nut filing.

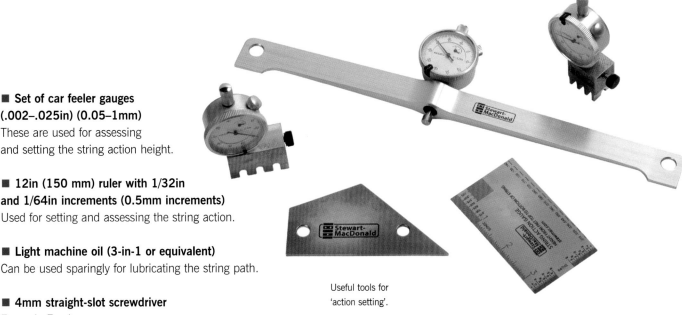

Useful tools for 'action setting'.

■ **Screw extractor HSS drills and tap wrenches**
For broken screws.

■ **Zap-It electric screwdriver attachment**
Makes light work of de-stringing guitars.

■ **Stewmac jack socket fixer**
Great for securing the traditional vintage Telecaster socket.

Consider also having a set of bench drawers and tidies for all those often misplaced odds and sods that are essential for guitar maintenance.

■ **Electronic tuner**
An accurate electronic tuner with a jack socket as opposed to an internal microphone will make short work of adjusting the intonation of individual string lengths.

■ **Wire cutters**
Useful for cutting strings to length. Overlong strings at the headstock are a safety hazard and tear up your gig bag.

■ **Peg winder**
Time saving, and avoids repetitive strain injury when changing strings. Fit one to your electric screwdriver.

■ **Polish and cloth**
A soft duster for the body and the back of the neck, and a lint-free cotton cloth for strings and fingerboard. Proprietary guitar polishes differ from household furniture polishes, which often contain silicone. The wax used in guitar polish is emulsified to avoid any sticky residue, especially under the heat generated by stage lighting.

■ **A small penlite torch**
Useful for closer examination of details. Useful at any time but especially in a stageside emergency.

✎ **Tech Tip**

When working on vintage brittle plastics consider using a fixed torque screwdriver – adjusted to avoid the kind of damage seen on many old guitars. Once set, these screwdrivers cannot over-tighten. The angled drivers are useful for 'awkward to reach' spots.

Henry Phillips

Have you ever wondered why Leo Fender and most guitar manufacturers switched to Phillips-type screws?

In the 1950s many fledgling companies were taking lessons from the streamlined assembly process at Henry Ford's car lines in Detroit. For these, Henry Phillips (1890–1958) had developed the cross-head screw. In 1936 The American Screw Co persuaded General Motors to use the Phillips-head screw in manufacturing Cadillacs, and by 1940 virtually every American automaker had switched to Phillips screws.

This new screw worked well with ratchet and electric screwdrivers, had greater torque, was self-centring, and didn't slip from the slot so easily, avoiding damage to the valuable paintjob. The speed with which Phillips screws can be used was crucial to the auto assembly line. In addition, Phillips screws are almost impossible to over-screw, which was very important.

However, cam-out or torque-out makes tightly driven Phillips screws fiendishly hard to remove and often damages the screw, the driver, and anything else a suddenly loose driver happens to hit. And whereas a coin or a piece of scrap metal can often be used to loosen a slot screw, nothing takes the place of a Phillips screwdriver. A flat-bladed driver or even a wrong-size Phillips just makes cam-out worse.

Beware: Phillips screwdrivers should not be used with Pozidrive screws (and vice versa). They are subtly different and when mixed they tend to ride out of the slot as well as rounding the corners of both the tool and screw recess.

■ Soldering iron
This should be at least 25W with a penlight tip. An iron is essential when replacing worn out volume pots and three-way switches etc. It's worth investing in a stand with a sponge cleaner attached (Draper components 23554 or similar). A crocodile clip multi-arm is also useful for holding small components in place.

■ A tube of solder
Multicore-type non-acid resin.

■ Tweezers
For rescuing dropped screws from awkward cavities and removing hot wires during soldering.

■ Crocodile clips
Can be used as isolating 'heat sinks' – but not too close to the joins, as they'll hamper the operation by drawing away too much heat.

■ Solder syringe
Makes light work of drawing old solder from previous electrical joints.

⚡ Tech Tip

The worst-case scenario with soldering is melting the plastic on interior wires – so be quick! But also keep the components steady: a wire moved while solder is setting may cause a 'dry joint' and poor conductivity.

John Diggins – Luthier

The insulated handles on these tools are soft rubber – less likely to scratch the guitar.

Useful accessories

- Vaseline or ChapStick for lubrication.
- Silicone or graphite locksmiths' nut lubricant.
- Matchsticks or cocktail sticks for lubrication application and 'rawlplugging' loose screws.
- Pipe cleaners and cotton buds for cleaning awkward spots; an old electric toothbrush can also be useful.
- Radius gauges for setting the bridge saddles.
- An electronic multimeter for testing pickup circuits.
- A set of socket spanners for removing and tightening pot nuts, jack sockets and some modern machine heads.
- Mechanical and digital callipers are great for all sorts of detailed measurements.
- Loctite or similar multi-purpose superglue.
- Craft knife for nut work.
- Thread gauges, useful for checking for correct threads on replacement screws etc.
- Rubber hammer, safer in many situations on valuable instruments.
- Wire stripper.
- Lemon oil for rosewood fingerboards.
- Spare jack socket, 250K pot, knobs and pickup switch.
- Dental abrasives and/or abrasive cord for fine-tuning a nut slot.

Fret tools

Diamond 'stones' for fret levelling, and bevelled-edge fret-shaping files are available, but these are specialist tools only needed for ambitious projects.

Working environment

Many guitar repairs and much maintenance can be safely carried out with the guitar resting in its hard shell case on a normal kitchen table or on a Workmate-type DIY bench, suitably padded. The photographs in this book were 80%

done at home on a Workmate. However, see page 73 for precautions regarding the inhalation of cellulose etc. Outside the guitar case environment, a small 1m square of carpet sample Blu-Tacked to a workbench can avoid a lot of inadvertent damage to guitar paintwork.

All the guitar techs and luthiers consulted for this book seemed to have their own ingenious home-made tools for some very specific jobs.

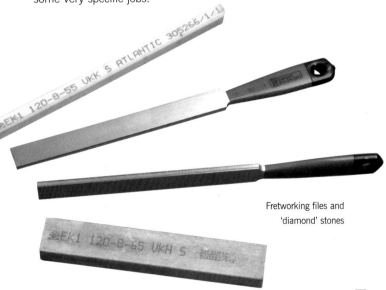

Fretworking files and 'diamond' stones

Essential gig bag accessories

Carrying a few spares can save you a long walk, but you have enough to carry to a gig without hauling your whole toolkit around. The mere essentials, compactly stowed, will potentially save a lot of pre-gig hassle, and should fit in your gig bag zip compartment.

Tech Tip

Beware of 'guitar multi-tools' – they look great in the shop, but most current models are difficult to use without damage to the guitar.

Frank Marvel

We suggest...

- A multipoint screwdriver with Phillips '0', '1' and '2' bits and small and medium point conventional straight-slot heads. The CruzTOOLS gig bag kit has '1' and '2' Phillips and 3mm and 6mm straight-slots. A straight-slot screwdriver is useful to have around for dealing with broken mains plugs and blown fuses.
- A small pair of wire snips for emergency string changes.
- Small 'emergency only' soldering iron and 6in of solder (not in the CruzTOOLS kit at present).
- Some 13A and 5A (UK) fuses, as well as any specific to your area of touring (*ie* USA and European equivalents, etc).
- A PP3 battery (for FX).
- A penlight torch.
- Spare plectrums and or finger picks.
- Allen/Hex keys for truss rod, etc.
- A nail file.
- A Leatherman or similar multitool – useful for a sharp blade and decent pliers.
- Insulating tape.
- Feeler gauges.
- A 6in rule.
- An electronic tuner.
- Spare strings.
- Plumbers PTFE tape – useful for securing loose control knobs.
- Bridge pin lever (found on most peg winders).

Unfortunately, by having this kit with you you'll acquire a reputation as Mr Ever Ready, and before long everybody in the band will come to depend on your tools!

It's worth doing a little maintenance

...Or getting an expert to do it for you. The electric guitar is proving to be a classic survivor. Even the rigours of the world tour have been surmounted with the help of a good flight case and a little loving care. Clearly few of us would risk taking a vintage guitar on the road, but barring abuse and given a few careful tweaks it would undoubtedly acquit itself well. A new guitar is also worth looking after, as a little effort can save embarrassing onstage failures.

Vintage antiques

If you're lucky enough to own a vintage guitar then what you have in your possession is not just a good instrument but a piece of popular music history. Given its rarity, you must regard the guitar as you would any other valuable 'antique'.

Whilst such guitars are considered a valuable investment, I personally share the view of many antique furniture collectors that design and function are part of the charm of such items and therefore they're best kept in use. I wonder about the 'investor' who thinks an instrument is best consigned to a bank vault. For me this seems a waste – like the owner who never actually drives his precious Ferrari. On visiting the world's museums I've observed that un-played instruments simply wilt and die. So I recommend that you enjoy your guitar whilst observing a few precautions:

- Never subject the instrument to any extremes of change in temperature and humidity. The chief victim here is the finish, which can crack or 'pave' as the underlying wood shrinks or expands. Vintage guitars are more prone to this as their paints and glazes are pervious – which may contribute to the character of their sound as the wood continues to 'breathe'.
- Give the instrument a good wipe down with a lint-free cloth after playing. This will reduce any damage to metal parts and finish caused by perspiration – the main cause of rust to the bridge and machine heads. This, of course, also preserves the strings, often doubling their useful life.
- Keep all the moving parts suitably lubricated.
- Use a good stable guitar stand. This sounds so obvious, but many once fabulous instruments turn up on the repair bench having been accidentally knocked off some precarious perch. Luthier John Diggins repairs one broken neck a month.

An Airline 2P Deluxe

Authenticity

Many used guitars have parts missing, particularly knobs and switches. It's perfectly natural to want to replace these. However, it's almost a custodial responsibility to replace these tastefully. These guitars will outlive us and carry on being worthwhile instruments for centuries. I predict the authentic 'early music' enthusiasts of 2050 will include people performing James Burton licks on authentic '50s Teles with vintage Fender amps. So seek out the most authentic replacement parts possible. It's relatively easy to buy 'aged' plastic parts with a suitable patina that ooze an atmosphere of smoky bars and long years on the chitlin circuit (see *Useful contacts* appendix). Do, however, make a careful note of any changes, as this will save arguments over authenticity at a later date.

Authenticity remains an issue 'under the hood', and with an old instrument it is extremely prudent to conserve any original cloth-covered wiring and even to use authentic '50s-type solders. This may sound over the top at present but the collectors and players of the next century will remember you warmly for taking that extra bit of trouble.

■ Keep the original parts

Over the years I have personally accumulated a small collection of bits from previous guitars, including a couple of bridge parts from a '62 Fiesta Red Strat, my first proper guitar. Now, in 1969 when I sold the guitar these seemed to be scrap metal and it never occurred to me to pass them on. But if the guitar still exists, and it probably does (serial no 87827 – let me know if you have it!), these old parts are an important part of what antiquarians call 'provenance'. A dealer may spot the 'new' saddle pieces I obtained with great difficulty in 1966, and wonder if the guitar really is a '62 Fiesta Red, but if the present owner had the old parts it completes a part of that story which supports the authenticity of the overall instrument. So put those old parts in a safe place and label them with any information you have.

An Encore starter kit – not a collector's item yet!

Stageside repairs

Given that the electric guitar always requires the rigging of an amp, tuning up and checking of leads et , it's worth arriving at a gig at least one hour before showtime. This allows for sound-checks and time for the things that inevitably go wrong to be put right. Sound-checks also give the PA man a chance to serve your needs better – to understand the likely combinations of instruments and any instrument changes during your set. Sound-checks are also great for finding solutions to the inevitable hiccups that arise in an unfamiliar venue.

No sound from your guitar – Step 1

- Don't panic! Work systematically through the cable chain, starting at the guitar, as the whole system is very unlikely to have failed completely.
- If possible try changing the pickup selector to another pickup. Is the volume control turned up?
- Still no sound? Try replacing the cable between the guitar and the amplifier with a new cable (one you're sure is working – for instance, the one another guitar player is already successfully using).
- The above step should bypass and eliminate any effects chain.
- If you then have sound, try reinserting the effects chain. (Still no sound? Go to Step 2).

- If you have sound then you merely had a faulty cable, the most common cause of on-stage sound failure. Never be tempted by the false economy of cheap cables – they always let you down by failing at critical moments, and can also affect your sound by introducing higher capacitance at certain frequencies. Buy reputable, rugged cables.
- If the sound fails again then it would seem the some component of the effects chain is faulty – work through the chain, replacing one cable at a time to (hopefully) isolate the fault.
- If cable replacement doesn't solve the problem try systematically removing one effect at a time from the chain.
- If you find a 'dead' component of the chain try replacing its associated battery or power supply.

No sound from your guitar – Step 2

- Still no sound, even though you're now plugged directly into the amplifier with a 'new' cable?
- The likely scenario is a 'failed' amplifier, so try checking the obvious causes such as:

- Has the volume been inadvertently turned down to zero? Check the master volume and all channel gains.
- Is the standby switch in the ON position?
- Does the mains light (if fitted) show 'ON'?
- Is the amplifier plugged into the mains? Is the mains switched on? Does the stage have a separate fuse?
- Are other amplifiers on the same circuit working?

- If yours is the only failed amp then look to the fuses. There are likely to be fuses on the amplifier (usually a screw-type fuse cartridge near the mains switch). There may also be fuses in the mains plug. Try replacements.
- If all of this fails then you must assume the amplifier has a *major* fault and try a 'work around' – *eg* sharing an amplifier with the other musicians etc. Any band should carry at least one spare amp.
- The crucial thing here is to be systematic – work through the chain logically, eliminating elements of the chain until the fault is isolated.

The guitar won't stay in tune?

Strings!

The most likely cause of tuning difficulties on an otherwise well-maintained guitar is poor or worn strings. The bad news is that changing strings one hour before a gig is also a formula for disaster, as the strings really need time to settle. In an emergency try replacing any individual strings that seem particularly troublesome – rusty or damaged strings inevitably cause severe tuning problems.

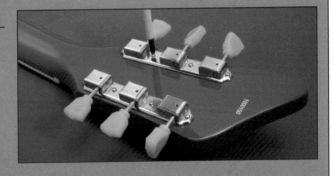

Loose components?

- Have the neck securing screws worked loose? A quarter-turn can improve the neck stability, but don't go mad – beware of cracking the surrounding lacquer by over-tightening.

- Are the machine heads loose?
NB: A machine head that's securely fitted but turns without altering pitch needs replacement. In practice this is unlikely to happen suddenly and should be picked up during routine maintenance.

- If the guitar has a vibrato fitted is it poorly set up? This is unlikely to respond to a quick fix.

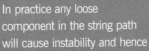

In practice any loose component in the string path will cause instability and hence tuning problems – examine the guitar for loose screws and lost or corroded securing springs. If the strings are OK and there are no obvious loose components, then perhaps you've changed string gauges without realigning the bridge intonation?

Replacing tuners

'Tuners', or machine heads, are one of the most mechanical elements of your guitar. They get heacy use and inevitably wear out. Also, many economy guitars are supplied with cheap, unreliable tuners that are worth upgrading.

Replacing Kluson vintage-type tuners

Fenders and Squiers are often fitted with Kluson-type semi-enclosed machine heads. These were the most easily available heads at the time of manufacture but are not perfect. They have a tendency to a 'dead spot' phenomenon, where turning the tuner in opposite directions often has no effect on the string post and therefore on the string tension. The dead spot is caused by poor manufacturing tolerances and the initial use of brass for the worm gear as opposed to steel.

Fortunately Spertzel and Gotoh now manufacture an exact lookalike with the advantage of a better gearing ratio – 15:1 rather than the vintage 12:1 – and come with nylon washers to take up any slack on the worm gear.

There may, however, be slight differences in the size of the bushings on replacements. The solution is to file the serrated teeth on the new bushings rather than deface the guitar.

1 First remove the strings. Always take the time to reduce the neck tension in a slow and methodical way to reduce the risk of upsetting the balance of the fixed neck.

2 The very old Kluson fixing screws require a straight-slot 4mm screwdriver for removal, and most post-'52 guitars a No '1' Phillips.

3 When positioning the new machine heads remember to replace the metal ferrules.

Keep old parts

To preserve its looks and value, when replacing any parts on a guitar always try to get the nearest you can to an identical replacement and store any vintage parts safely. They will help provide provenance for the instrument at any future sale.

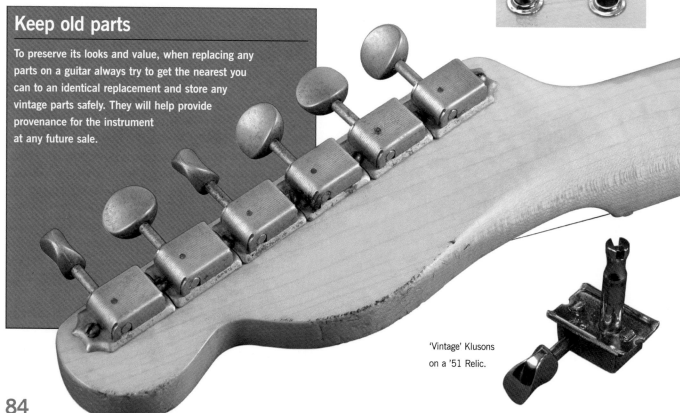

'Vintage' Klusons on a '51 Relic.

Replacing 'LP' and other three-a-side tuners

Most early 'LP' types were fitted with John Kluson's 1938-patented enclosed tuners. More recently the Grover brand has been adopted for most new Gibson and Epiphone models and many other brands. Replacement is usually a quite straightforward 'one for one' operation. I would recommend sticking to Kluson types on any vintage guitar – they're even available with aged 'tulip' tuners to keep the vibe of an old guitar.

Replacing Kluson three-a-side-type tuners

1 First remove the strings. Always take the time to reduce the neck tension in a slow and methodical way to reduce the risk of upsetting the balance of the fixed neck.

2 For removal the old Kluson fixing screws require a No '0' or '1' Phillips screwdriver.

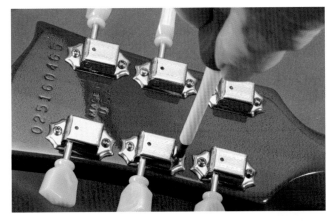

3 Remember to replace the metal ferrules.

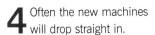

4 Often the new machines will drop straight in.

Sometimes the new ferrules are bigger than the originals, and if this is the case you might want to refer any redrilling to a qualified luthier, especially when working on a rare and valuable guitar.

Replacing Grovers

These are common on many modern 'LP' types, including some Epiphone models. The changing procedure is as above, except for the extra removal of the locking nut, which often requires a 10mm socket spanner.

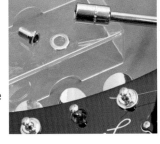

1 The Grover rear screw is another No '1' Phillips.

2 The replacements should drop into place without any need for adjustment to the ferule holes.

3 Don't forget the washer when replacing the locking ferrule. Tighten the locking nut with a 10mm socket spanner, ensuring a good tight fit – crucial to tuning stability.

Pickup height settings: tone and intonation

It is reasonable to assume that having the pickups set high and therefore closer to the strings will produce more output from your guitar and possibly more tone. However, be aware that the magnetic field from your pickups is strong enough to interfere with the natural excursion of the strings, which can result in very odd harmonic effects. Most notably the sixth string sounded at the 12th fret can produce odd 'beats' and very uneven intonation.

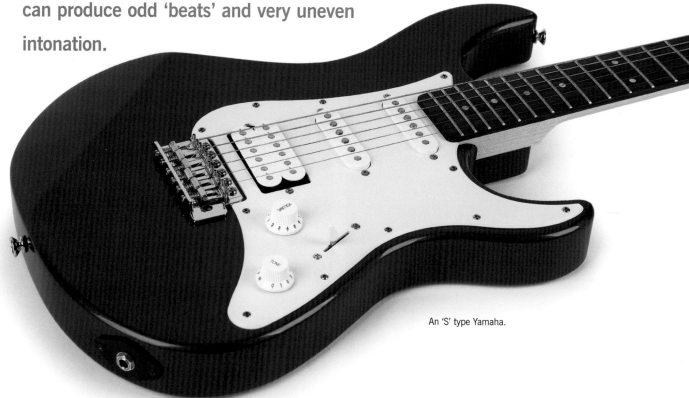

An 'S' type Yamaha.

'S' and 'T' types (single coil and humbuckers)

1 Depress all of the strings at the last fret. Using a 6in (150mm) ruler or a string action gauge (handily marked up in 64ths), measure the distance from the bottom of the first and sixth strings to the top of the pole piece. As a rule of thumb, the distance should be greatest at the sixth string, for the neck pickup position, and closest at the first string, for the bridge pickup position.

Follow the measurement guidelines in the Fender chart below as a starting point – even if your guitar isn't a Fender, the pickups are likely to be similar. The distance will vary according to the amount of magnetic pull of your specific pickup.

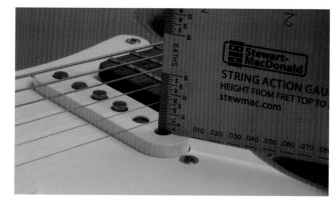

In the last analysis you'll have to decide for yourself on the most effective compromise between output and magnetic interference.

Fender recommendations as a guide:

	Bass side	Treble side
Texas Specials	8/64in (3.6mm)	6/64in (2.4mm)
Vintage style	6/64in (2.4mm)	5/64in (2mm)
Humbuckers	4/64in (1.6mm)	4/64in (1.6mm)

2 Using a No '2' Phillips screwdriver and an accurate metal ruler, adjust the height to the recommended starting point.
Be aware that when lowering the pickup extensively the pickup screw sometimes becomes disengaged from its socket. Consequently this procedure isn't recommended just before a gig, as relocating the screw usually means removing the pickguard!

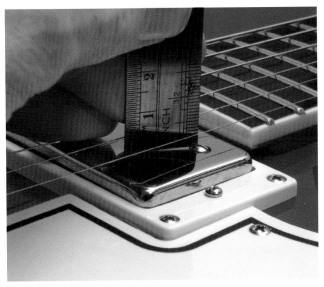

Again you'll have to decide for yourself on the most effective compromise between output level, tone and magnetic interference.

Humbucker height recommendations

	Bass side	Treble side
Neck pickup	3/32in	1/16in
Bridge pickup	3/32in	1/16in

2 Using a No '1' Phillips screwdriver and an accurate metal ruler, adjust the height to the above starting points and then follow Gibson's own idea of adjusting for your sound.

Gibson 'LP' type and other humbuckers

Gibson, who introduced the humbucker, have an interesting recommendation for humbuckers, which is not height specific but is based on listening. They suggest that having your pickups set too high will cause a muddy, overly distorted sound, and having them set too low will produce a weak, unfocused sound. So they suggest either leaving the pickups at their 'optimally set' factory height or experimenting by ear until you find the sound that works for you!

1 To establish your current setting, depress all of the strings at the last fret. Using a 6in (150mm) ruler, measure the distance from the bottom of the first and sixth strings to the top of the pole piece. As a rule of thumb, the distance should be greatest at the sixth string, for the neck pickup position, and closest at the first string position.
A guide figure based on factory-set Gibsons would be bridge pickup 3/32in at the sixth string and 1/16in at the first.

Jack socket maintenance or replacement

Heavy use of your guitar may result in electrical 'crackling'. If this is the case try adjusting the tension on the spring steel jack retainer.

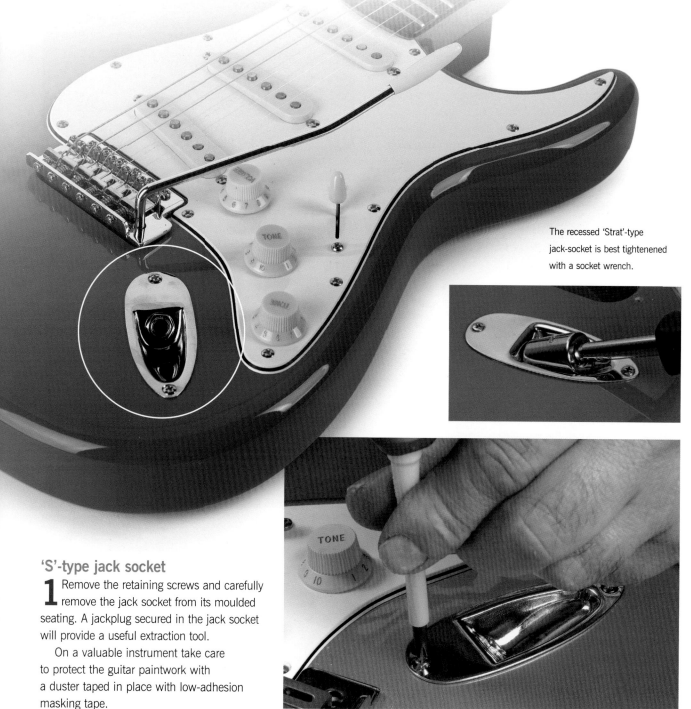

The recessed 'Strat'-type jack-socket is best tightenened with a socket wrench.

'S'-type jack socket

1 Remove the retaining screws and carefully remove the jack socket from its moulded seating. A jackplug secured in the jack socket will provide a useful extraction tool.

On a valuable instrument take care to protect the guitar paintwork with a duster taped in place with low-adhesion masking tape.

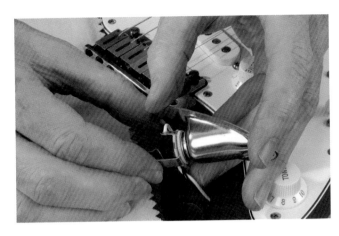

2 A gentle squeeze of the spring steel jack retainer may restore the required electrical contact sufficiently. Check for corrosion on any metal parts. If possible clean any corrosion using a little lighter fuel on a cotton bud. If the jack socket seems beyond repair then consider fitting an approved replacement. This may be a little more expensive than a cheap jack socket from a radio repair shop but it will be the right size and is likely to be more suitably robust. All jack sockets are not created equal.

5 Solder the new jack socket, retaining the tip and sleeve polarity as per your labelling. **NB:** Use 0.32in 60/40 rosin-core electrical solder and a pen-type iron rated at 25W and above.

3 REPLACEMENT – IF REQUIRED. If in any doubt label the cables as 'tip' and 'sleeve'. Then carefully melt the solder joins and remove the old jack socket.

6 Rebolt the jack socket in position and refit the chrome retainer.

4 Remove the jack socket from the moulded chrome retainer by unscrewing the outer nut. You can find the correct socket size by trial an error or by referring to the appropriate case studies in this book.

'LP' and some modern 'T' types

1 Remove the four Phillips No '1' screws attaching the jack socket.

2 A gentle squeeze of the 'earth' springed connector may suffice to give a little more tension to the socket.

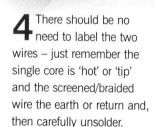

4 There should be no need to label the two wires – just remember the single core is 'hot' or 'tip' and the screened/braided wire the earth or return and, then carefully unsolder.

■ If the jack still seems a little loose then it's worth replacing it with a high-quality guitar-type socket – one that's designed to take regular use. It's worth paying a little extra for a quality component that won't let you down in a pressured stage environment.

5 Solder the new socket in place, retaining the correct polarity as per your labelling.

NB: Use 0.32in 60/40 rosin-core electrical solder and a small iron rated at 25W and above.

3 Removing the old socket first by loosening the retaining nut with a (12mm) socket spanner avoids possible heat damage to the plastic retaining panel. Nut sizes will vary.

6 Rebolt the jack in place and replace the four Phillips screws on the mounting plate. Take care not to twist the wires as you reinsert the socket.

Vintage cool – 'T' type sockets

If you wish to preserve the integrity of an 'original' socket on a vintage 'T'-type guitar, stewmac.com supply a brilliant little gizmo for revitalising the grip of an old retainer clip. This is the 'Tele Jack Installation Tool', which expands the clip so that its corners bite into the walls of the jack cavity.

Stewmac Tele jack installation tool.

1 Place a pre-bent retainer clip over the bolt with its wings pointing out of the guitar socket – the retainer clip slots into the special nut. Screw the lower part of the tool on to the bolt, just enough to retain the 'retainer' but not flatten it!

2 Insert it into the guitar and tighten with the supplied 8mm Allen wrench. Keep the bolt from revolving using a suitable 22mm or adjustable spanner. Note the low-adhesion masking tape on the guitar body.

3 When the retainer feels secure remove the bolt by unscrewing the Allen wrench, thus freeing the tool from the cavity.

NB: If the hole containing the jack cup has been badly damaged by the old retaining clip, you can rebuild the wall of the hole with a mixture of Araldite two-pack resin and sawdust. Dried out, this works like a new wood surface and the replacement clip bites.

Extracting a distorted or loose retainer

Note that the 'Tele-Jack' tool can also be used in reverse. Used this way it collapses an old retainer clip, making it easy to remove. (There are detailed notes with the tool.)

Archtops

For tips on archtop jack socket retrieval and access see page 104.

Replacing volume and tone controls

The principal elements are the same for most electric guitars
but the access procedure and pot values differ.

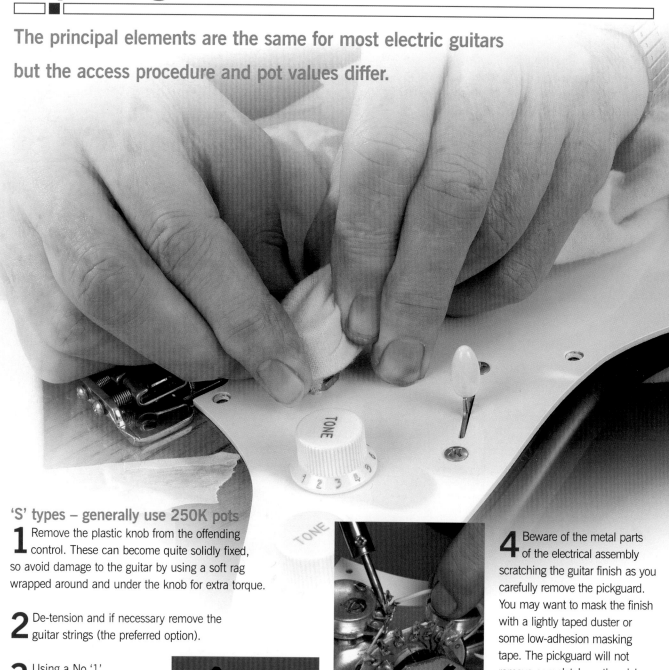

'S' types – generally use 250K pots

1 Remove the plastic knob from the offending
control. These can become quite solidly fixed,
so avoid damage to the guitar by using a soft rag
wrapped around and under the knob for extra torque.

2 De-tension and if necessary remove the
guitar strings (the preferred option).

3 Using a No '1'
Phillips screwdriver,
unscrew the pickguard
and keep the screws
together in a small
container (an aerosol
cap is perfect).

4 Beware of the metal parts
of the electrical assembly
scratching the guitar finish as you
carefully remove the pickguard.
You may want to mask the finish
with a lightly taped duster or
some low-adhesion masking
tape. The pickguard will not
remove completely as the pickup
wiring is soldered to the output
jack. It's usually worth separating
the pickup assembly completely
by carefully unsoldering the
output jack at the pickup end –
usually attached to the back of
the volume pot.

5 Before unsoldering, label the cables connected to the old pot with some cloth-backed tape ('cloth-backed' is easy to write on, though a sticky label wrapped back on itself works just as well), assign each cable a number, and draw yourself a little sketch of what

goes where, noting the orientation of the tags on the old pot in relationship to the back of the pickguard. This sounds elementary, but some old cables are not colour coded and there are alternative wiring options. Taking this approach restores your wiring intact and gets you back to the sound you've come to expect.

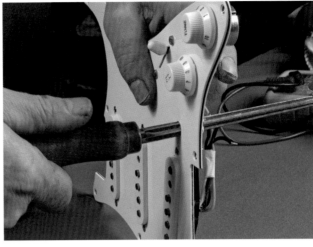

6 Place a crocodile clip or similar on the wiring between the pot and the pickups to act as a 'heat sink', absorbing heat that might otherwise find itself cooking your pickups. Carefully unsolder the old pot with the lowest rating soldering iron you have – 15W may work but a higher rated iron used quickly will be fine.

8 Sometimes the new pot has a slightly larger shank, in which case you'll need to enlarge the pickguard hole with a rat tail file or similar.

9 Place the new pot in position, retaining the old orientation (refer to your diagram), and fix with the new retaining nut.

7 Use a socket-type spanner – the size will vary from model to model (see *Case studies* on pages 124–176) – to unbolt the nut retaining the pot to the pickguard. (A socket-type spanner is less likely to mark the pickguard.)

Protect your eyes

Replacing volume or tone controls involves electrical soldering, so protect your eyes with safety glasses and cover any guitar parts that may be spattered by stray solder.

10 Tin the new connecting tags for the replacement pot with a little solder and solder them in place as per your labelling. A lollipop stick makes an effective aid and also doesn't waste any heat. Reassemble as before.

'LP' types – generally use 500K pots

1 Remove the plastic knob from the offending control. These can become quite solidly fixed, so avoid damage to the guitar by using a soft rag wrapped around and under the knob for extra torque.

2 Using a No '1' Phillips screwdriver, unscrew the rear panel and keep the screws together in a small container.

3 Label the cables connected to the old pot with some cloth-backed tape Assign each cable a number, and draw yourself a little sketch of what goes where, noting the orientation of the tags on the old pot in relationship to the back of the pickguard. This sounds elementary, but some old cables are not colour coded and there are alternative wiring options. Taking this approach restores your wiring intact.

4 Carefully unsolder the old pot with the lowest rating soldering iron you have – 15W may work but a higher rated iron used quickly will be fine.

5 Use a socket-type spanner – the size will vary from model to model (see *Case studies* on pages 124–176) – and unbolt the nut retaining the pot to the guitar body. (A socket-type spanner/wrench is less likely to mark the lacquer than a conventional spanner and any abrasion is below the switch skirt.)

6 Place the new pot in position, retaining the old orientation (refer to your diagram), and fix with the new retaining nut.

7 Tin the new connecting wires for the replacement pot with a little solder and solder them in place as per your labelling. A crocodile-clip stand makes a great 'third hand' for these jobs. A lollipop stick also works as a non-conductive aid and doesn't waste any heat. Reassemble as before.

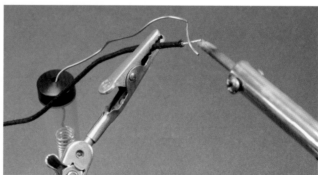

'T' types and others

Generally single-coils are associated with 250K pots and humbuckers with 500K. Access on 'T' types is easy as the pots and switch have their own dedicated panel, easily removed and attached with two No '1' Phillips screws.

Semi-acoustics

The replacement principles are the same as for the 'LP' type but with generally more difficult access. For hints on dealing with the access problems, see page 104.

94

Replacing pickup selectors

The pickups Leo Fender and Gibson designers chose were fairly rugged and took the pressure. However, price competition has recently driven manufacturers to use very flimsy components and these are worth replacing.

Replacing an 'S'-type five-way selector

A replacement Fender five-way switch (PN 017053) is readily available from suppliers and will fit into most existing pickguard slots without any modification. You may, however, want to consider the Schaller equivalent, which offers pickups one and three combined as well! (See *Useful contacts* appendix.) Place the guitar on a protective surface. An old blanket on a sturdy table or workbench is ideal.

1 Remove the plastic control knob from the existing selector switch. This is a push fit and should come away easily.

3 Carefully remove the pick guard screws with a No '1' Phillips screwdriver. Store the screws in a plastic aerosol lid.

2 Remove the guitar strings, one at a time and working towards the middle – *ie* take the sixth and first strings off, then second and fifth, etc, so that the strain loss on the neck is even and gradual. Though many experienced guitar techs remove all the strings at once with a set of wire cutters, they can solve all the problems this potentially causes relatively quickly, whereas you probably don't have that skill and experience. I therefore recommend the slower and more stable approach.

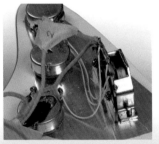

4 Carefully remove the pickguard, ensuring you don't put undue strain on the electrical loom and that you avoid causing any damage as you ease the guard from under the extended fingerboard.

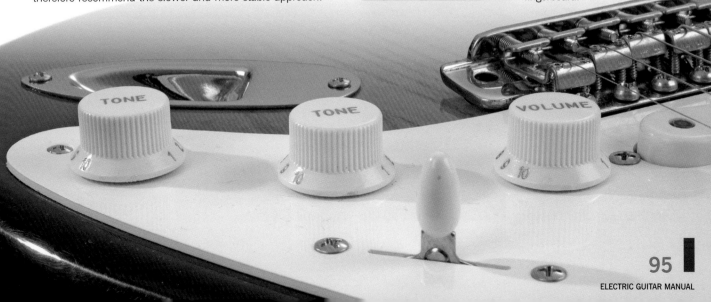

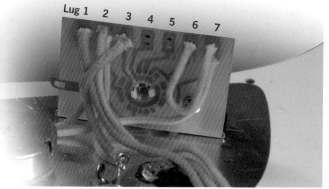

Figure 1

Neck tone control

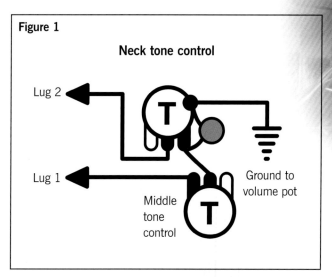

Lug 2

Lug 1

T

T

Middle tone control

Ground to volume pot

8 Carefully resolder the existing wires following the switch diagram above or your custom diagram. Use a minimum of solder and contact the components with the iron for just long enough to heat the solder. There are options on the pickup selections available and the tone control allocation. These depend on the make and model of the replacement switch, so follow the suppliers' guidelines.

5 If you find the diagram above easy to follow, fine. If not, label your existing wires 1, 2, 3, 4, 5 and 6 and draw yourself a custom diagram that you can comfortably follow. Carefully unsolder the old three-pole switch.

6 Protecting the guitar finish with a carefully placed duster or masking tape, slowly unscrew the old switch mounting screws using a No '1' or '2' Phillips screwdriver (depending on the model). Rushing this process will inevitably damage some of the

screw edge and eventually make the screws difficult to remove. Taking out the screws slowly and firmly will avoid slippage and you're less likely to scratch the pickguard. Note the position of the old switch – which side is the fibre insulation?

9 Replace the pickguard in position and carefully screw it down. **NB:** Do not over-tighten the pickguard screws, as the plastic – particularly on the single-ply pickguards – is easily cracked.

10 Restring the guitar, first and sixth strings first, etc, as before, and gradually ease up to full tension. With luck the guitar neck will go back to its former position. If not, refer to the relevant set-up section on page 62.

7 Place the new switch in position, taking care to ensure it is the same way up as your original – which side is the insulation? Screw the switch in place using the existing screws. Tin the new switch connections with a minimum of solder.

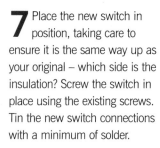

11 Test the new switching. A tuning fork held over the pickups easily indicates which pickups are on in which selector position. You should get:

Position 1	Bridge pickup only.
Position 2	Bridge and middle.
Position 3	Middle only. (The Schaller E Model Mega switch option gives neck and bridge.)
Position 4	Middle and neck.
Position 5	Neck only.

Replacing an 'LP' or 'SG'-type three-way selector

This type is also found on the 330, 335 and many other archtops.

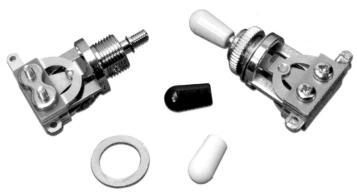

Bear in mind that three-way switches on Gibson and Epiphone models differ in quality and in thread sizes. For instance, if you wish to replace the plastic knob on the American guitars the thread is 32G 5/32in, available from Switchcraft, and on Epiphones 40G 1/8in.

The Epiphone Standard we're using here comes from China with a short, and often short-lived, three-way switch that is well worth replacing. The longer barrelled professional-type switch usually found on Gibson Les Pauls is readily available and less prone to intermittence and 'crackle and pop'. It will fit in the cavity on most Epiphones.

1 Remove the switch rear access hatch with a No '1' Phillips.

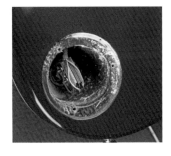

2 Remove the knurled retaining ring using this specially designed tool or a pair of suitably 'softened' pliers (try some masking tape on the jaws).

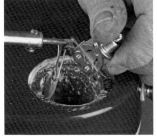

3 Unsolder the old switch (labelling the wires if you're in any doubt as to their orientation). If, like me, you're a less than professional electrician then protect the guitar from solder with a suitably placed cloth.

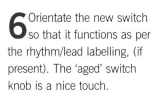

4 Unscrew the knurled ring from the new switch.

5 Position the new switch and resolder.

6 Orientate the new switch so that it functions as per the rhythm/lead labelling, (if present). The 'aged' switch knob is a nice touch.

NB: Replacement on hollow body guitars is more complicated – see page 104 for tips and advice.

Replacing a 'T'-type selector

The procedure is much as the 'S' type, though 'T' types most often have a three-way switch. Access and replacement is easy due to the simple 'T'-type control panel.

Pickup replacement

Given a guitar with the right components and body type the most crucial factor in achieving an authentic sound has to be getting the pickups right.

One of the truly wonderful developments of the last few decades has to be the appearance of dozens of specialist pickup manufacturers. These companies don't just offer highly accurate reproductions of all the vintage classic pickups, but also provide a plethora of variations and developments in both passive and active options.

Over the page are procedures for two standard replacement upgrades and one classic installation of the 'correct' pickup type in a lookalike guitar.

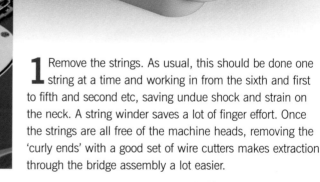

'S'-type upgrade: fitting Texas Specials

There are many replacement pickup options, but as we're dealing with the 'S'-type guitar I'll provide details of the most popular change. This entails fitting Fender Texas Specials to a budget Squier guitar. These slightly overwound pickups are based on those used by Stevie Ray Vaughan, and feature in the SRV Fender guitar. They're available from Fender dealers and come as a matched set of three, complete with all the wiring, screws and pickup covers you're likely to need.

1 Remove the strings. As usual, this should be done one string at a time and working in from the sixth and first to fifth and second etc, saving undue shock and strain on the neck. A string winder saves a lot of finger effort. Once the strings are all free of the machine heads, removing the 'curly ends' with a good set of wire cutters makes extraction through the bridge assembly a lot easier.

2 Unscrew the scratchplate with a No '1' Phillips screwdriver and put the screws aside in a plastic retainer or similar. Many modern 'S' types feature an extra fret, which means that care must be taken manoeuvring the scratchplate from under the lip that extends the fingerboard an extra quarter-inch or so to accommodate this additional fret.

3 Make a careful note of where your original pickup wires are connected – label the wires if necessary.

■ Following Leo Fender's original design concept, you can now remove the complete pickup and electrics assembly by simply desoldering the jack socket, pickup selector connections and tremolo earth/ground wires.

■ For this you'll need a 25W soldering iron, an iron stand and a wet sponge for removing redundant solder from the iron.

■ When removing the wires from the back of the control pots and pickup selector be as quick as possible, to avoid any heat damage.

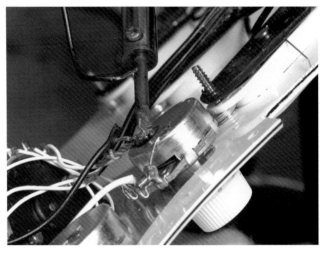

4 Remove the trem ground wire at the pickup end as this will be easier – the trem end requires a bigger, hotter iron. Having separated the pickup/scratchplate assembly put the neck body assembly in a safe place and continue.

5 Fender supply a clear diagram with their Texas Specials indicating the correct wiring arrangement, which assumes you have a standard five-way Fender switch installed. However, since you may not have this switch it's doubly important that you now label all your wires before removal. Separate the pickup wiring loom with a sharp craft knife.

6 With a Phillips No '1' screwdriver, carefully remove the old pickups. Note the original equipment has metal springs to facilitate adjustment of the pickup heights. However, the Texas Specials and most top-of-the-range Strats feature soft latex washers in this role. John Diggins tells me that this is probably because the latex washers afford better acoustic damping than springs. The snag, though, is that they naturally perish over time. However, I'll assume you're going to use the supplied authentic latex option.

7 Carefully install the new pickups using the latex washers.

■ Note that the new pickups have authentic old-fashioned but wonderfully useful 'waxed' wire. Carefully remove all the modern cheap and nasty vinyl wire during your installation. An advantage of the old-fashioned stuff is that it's 'push back' wire, enabling you to push the insulation back to expose the conductor for easy soldering.

■ Also note that the pickups are colour coded to identify their position – this is critical to the intended sound. Note particularly that the middle pickup is wired out of phase to aid a certain humbucking quality when the pickups are paired.

8 Mould the new wire into a neat loom and trim to the required length.

10 Solder the 'hot' wires (white) to the pickup selector according to your previous labelling.

NB: These connections are critical to retain the correct order of pickup selection.

9 All three black common ground wires can be soldered together to the back of the volume pot. A wooden lollipop stick makes a good heat-insulating tool for holding the wires in place.

The finished solder joint should be bright and shiny, indicating a good conducting medium – a 'dry' joint will be dull, indicating potential problem.

11 Carefully tape your pickup looms using masking tape.

12 Reassemble your completed pickup rig as originally found. This will entail restoring the trem ground/earth wire and the jack socket connections as per your original labelled connections.

'LP' humbucker-type pickup replacement

For replacement in an Epiphone Standard or similar guitar, I have chosen Seymour Duncan SH2 'Jazz' humbuckers in a matched pair, one for the bridge and a slightly different specification for the neck:

Alnico V Bar Magnets

	Neck	Bridge
DC resistance	7.72k	7.90k
Resonant peak	8kHz	7kHz

The relatively high resonant peaks should complement the Epiphone's alder body and maple top. The 'Jazz' title refers to the pickup's moderate output and clearer top end response. Seymours recommend this pickup for blues, country and classic rock and describe it as 'the consummate neck humbucker'. The four-wire pickup has been chosen to enable versatility of output wiring.

I'm keeping the covers on these pickups because I like the warmer sound that imparts. However, Mike Bloomfield and Jimmy Page preferred them off (just the bridge pickup in Jimmy's case). This alters the 'stray inductance' factor, accentuating the higher frequencies; but we also have EQ available on our amps for that so I decided to protect the fragile coils.

1 De-string the guitar. Release the tension on the neck evenly, *ie* first string/sixth string, fifth string/second string etc. This is particularly important on a set-neck guitar as neck resetting is a major and expensive job. If you have

Grover machines don't forget to loosen the tension screws before unwinding. An electric string winder attachment is a useful RSI buster. Plug in your soldering iron to warm up.

2 Remove the cover from the rear access panel using a No '1' Phillips screwdriver. Use a screw keep of some kind to avoid lost or mixed-up screws – I currently use recycled dental floss containers.

3 Remove the old pickups using the same screwdriver on the four mounting screws located at each corner. Place the mounting blocks to one side as these will fit the replacements perfectly. Note the slimmer mount for the neck pickup and the tapered angle – you'll need to retain this orientation on reassembly.

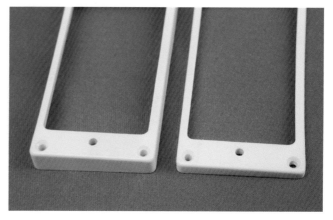

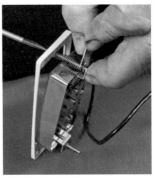

4 Draw yourself a diagram of the pickup wires' position in the existing arrangement. Then carefully snip off or unsolder the old pickup wiring from the existing volume pots. These connections can be identified from the wiring diagram (see below) or simply by gently tugging the pickup wires from the pickup cavity end.

5 Place the new pickups in the mounting blocks, taking care to observe the manufacturers' marked designation of 'neck' and 'bridge' pickup – they're electrically different; also take care to use the slimmer block for the neck pickup. John Diggins has a useful gizmo for holding the fiddly springs in place, but you can improvise.

6 Label the new pickup wires clearly, as once they're both in the control cavity they may appear to be the same. Put the neck pickup in place first as this makes wiring simpler. Carefully thread the cables through to the control cavity. Note the orientation of the pole pieces closest to the fingerboard when positioning the pickup.

7 Tin the new wires with a little solder and then resolder these as per your diagram, or use the diagram (left) as a guide. Replace the rear cavity cover.

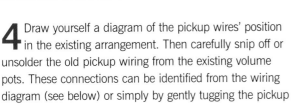

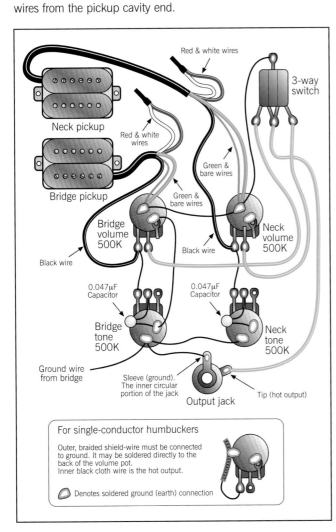

Red & white wires

Neck pickup

Red & white wires

Bridge pickup

Green & bare wires

Green & bare wires

3-way switch

Bridge volume 500K

Neck volume 500K

Black wire

Black wire

0.047µF Capacitor

0.047µF Capacitor

Bridge tone 500K

Neck tone 500K

Ground wire from bridge

Sleeve (ground). The inner circular portion of the jack

Output jack

Tip (hot output)

For single-conductor humbuckers

Outer, braided shield-wire must be connected to ground. It may be soldered directly to the back of the volume pot.
Inner black cloth wire is the hot output.

◯ Denotes soldered ground (earth) connection

Authentic sound from a copy guitar

The Ibanez Artcore featured in the case study on page 144 is very close to an authentic Gretsch Rockabilly guitar in many crucial ways. The body size and depth, scale length and vibrato unit all point in the direction of a Gretsch White Falcon, and the finish and set-up are remarkable. However, the pickups are of a type more associated with a Gibson PAF sound.

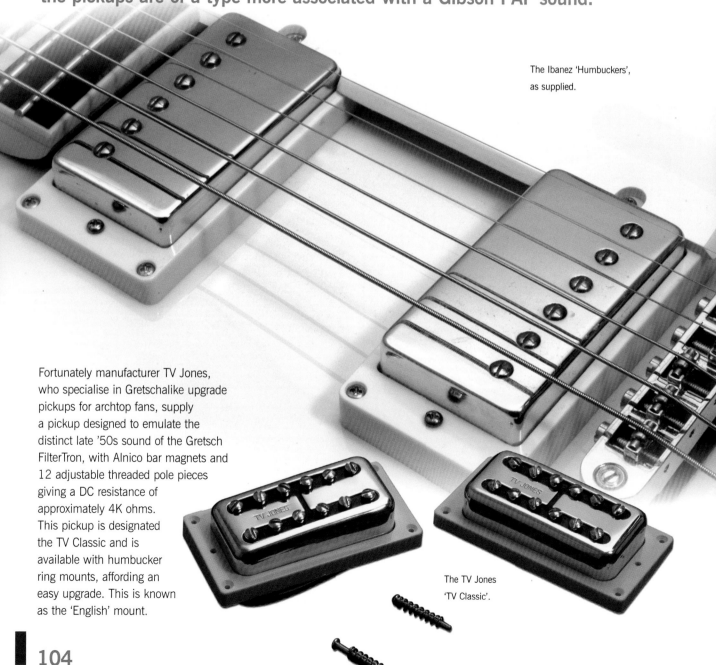

The Ibanez 'Humbuckers', as supplied.

Fortunately manufacturer TV Jones, who specialise in Gretschalike upgrade pickups for archtop fans, supply a pickup designed to emulate the distinct late '50s sound of the Gretsch FilterTron, with Alnico bar magnets and 12 adjustable threaded pole pieces giving a DC resistance of approximately 4K ohms. This pickup is designated the TV Classic and is available with humbucker ring mounts, affording an easy upgrade. This is known as the 'English' mount.

The TV Jones 'TV Classic'.

Installation

1 Lightly mark up the current bridge position with a soft pencil, as the bridge will move without string tension.

4 Label the four controls to avoid confusion and make a note of which pot is which. I've superglued the numbers on!

2 Strip the guitar strings observing the usual cautions (first string/sixth string, fifth string/second string etc). The scratchplate requires a No '1' Phillips screwdriver.

3 The old pickups are also removed with a No '1' Phillips.

5 I'm going to loosen the whole electric harness including the jack socket, but for ease of reassembly will attach thin nylon fishing line to each component before dropping it into the guitar, except for the jack socket, which is on a length of cord.

6 The pots and switch all require a socket spanner (14mm and 11mm in this case).

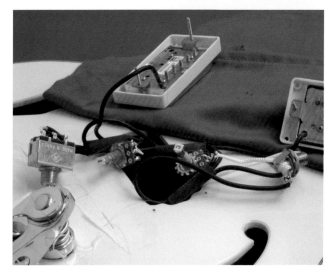

7 The key components can now be accessed via the pickup mounting hole. Make a written note of the old pickup connections.

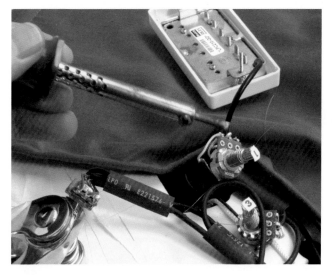

8 Carefully unsolder the old pickups.

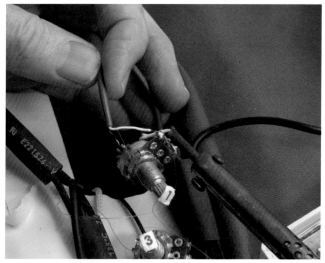

9 Trace the path of the pickup cable and make sure your new path is *exactly the same* – it's all too easy to get the pickups correctly soldered up but in such a way that they can't go back into the correct cavities, so BEWARE!

When you're sure you have a workable arrangement of cables solder the new pickup connections in place. Pre-tinning the wires with a little solder will make things easier.

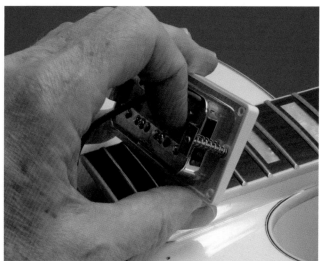

10 When installing the pickups check the orientation of the pickup mounts – they're not symmetrical! Also install the height adjusting springs.

11 A slight snag is that the new pickup-surround screw holes don't quite line up with the existing holes in the guitar – fortunately, however, the old holes will be invisible beneath the pickguard. If the pickup lines up OK then proceed. Otherwise you should fill the old holes with wood filler and relocate the pickup.

12 You'll need to pilot drill any new holes with a bit 0.5mm smaller than the new screws. The electrician's tape acts as a depth gauge. The new screws should now go in without cracking any lacquer (or polyurethane).

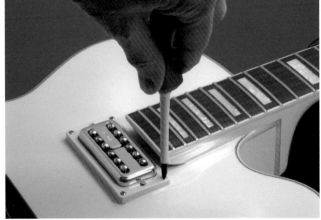

13 Repeat the process for the bridge pickup. Then pull the jack cord to relocate the jack, and fix it in place.

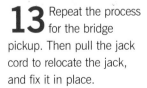

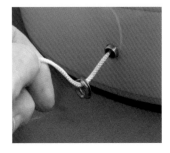

14 Follow the same procedure for the three-way switch and the volume and tone pots. The thin nylon thread makes relocating the switches and pots possible.

This replacement job is a fiddly and time-consuming process with a lot of frustrating 'try again' moments. Groping inside the F hole I managed to impale my finger on one of the pot prongs and it got stuck inside the guitar! However, the end result looks good and it sounds just like a 1960s Gretsch. Not as mellow as the original humbuckers, and with that quirky high-mid 'accent' that instantly identifies this type of guitar, great for early Beatles riffs and rockabilly twang. The guitar has gone from a 'jazzbox' to a rock'n'roll icon. Total outlay with guitar was about £500, whereas a branded guitar would be £2,000.

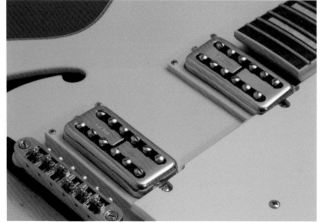

A little fretwork

The work shown here was done on an 'S' type, but the same techniques are applicable to most guitars. However, some 'LP' types have bound fingerboards that may introduce an extra complication and are not a DIY job.

This particular 'S' type is not unusual in having been poorly set up, as well as having a slightly unfinished feel to the frets and fingerboard. This is luthier John Diggins' solution, as taught to a willing apprentice.

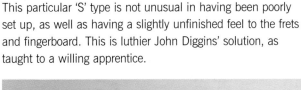

1 Check the removed neck for excessive relief using an accurate straight edge.

2 A quarter-turn right with a 5mm Allen key corrects the concave tendency.

3 A 'fret rocker' reveals any proud frets.

4 A diamond dressing stone is used to take the top of the proud frets, The firm sponge prevents any tendency for downward pressure to bend the neck. Constant checking with the straight edge is essential.

5 Some protrusion of the fret edges due to wood shrinkage is also dressed. A little masking tape acts as a useful guide and avoids accidentally damaging the urethane.

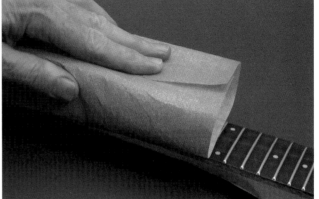

6 The 'flattened' frets are now restored to the correct contour with a large Stewmac fret file (John and I prefer to use the large file for both Gibson and Fender frets and customise the fret contour by hand). Both sides of the fret are contoured.

9 A further polish with fine abrasive 3M paper improves the feel...

7 The frets are then polished both ways, initially with 400 freecut paper and a soft-backed sanding block, then 1200 grit 'wet and dry'.

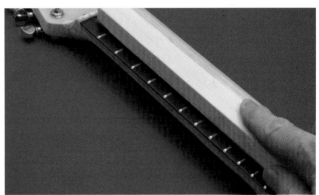

10 A final polish with a buffing wheel is ideal but a very good finish can be had with an old leather belt glued to a 2in x 1in baton and a little metal polish.

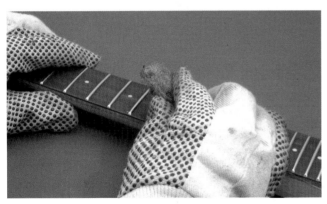

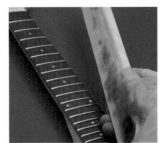

8 The rosewood needs a little finishing with some 0000 grade wire wool. Take care to use protective gloves!

11 A little lemon oil cleans and restores the fingerboard – the Dunlop type has its own useful built-in applicator.

'Serve and protect': caring for your axe

Many guitars arrive these days in a simple cardboard box that serves its purpose – as protection during the trip from the factory. However, as soon as you venture out with your new guitar, to your first rehearsal or a friend's party, you'll need to get yourself a decent gig bag. You should consider getting a hard case as soon as you start regular gigging.

Gig bags

These are great if you are carrying the guitar and nobody else is involved – you'll look after the guitar, because it's yours and you know it's fairly fragile. However, gig bags fall down as a means of protection when other people become involved: drivers will throw a gig-bagged guitar in the trunk of a car and drummers will stack stuff on top of it – it happens!

Some gig bags are better than others. The thin unpadded types offer minimal protection, while the heavily padded types offer a little more. However, if you're gigging with a band get a case! It's usually 'somebody else' who drops your guitar – usually a well-intentioned 'helping hand'.

Lightweight cases

Light cases made of fabric with a foam lining are ideal if you're responsible for your guitar and know who's doing the stacking. They certainly offer more protection than a gig bag, without the weight of a hardshell case, and are a good compromise. To provide the best protection the form-fit interior should be a cosy fit (unlike this one).

Multi-purpose hardshell cases

These are less expensive than the form-fit variety but take up more room in the van. But they're fairly rugged and will survive 12 months roadie abuse. Hiscox do a good range and can accommodate even the less common guitar shapes. Their Lite Flite cases are particularly good at thermal insulation, which is very important when going from a hot stage to a cold van. You need to avoid unintentionally 'relicing' your guitar by keeping its temperature and humidity stable.

Form-fit cases

Associated with brand names, these are often slightly more rugged and tend to have more robust clasps and hinges. In addition their exact fit affords more protection, and they take up less room in the van.

Tweed period cases

These are really for collectors and display purposes. On the road they soon get badly marked and shabby, and their weight won't make you any friends. But they do look cool!

Flight cases

If you're on tour or travelling by air then the flight case is the only real option for any hope of protection. An airline actually bought me this one after they totalled my form-fit hardcase. This is a 'full-flight' specification job and has provision for locking. There are cheap cases out there made of aluminium that look like flight cases but don't really do the job – so pay a premium price and see your guitar survive.

ABS flight cases

These are lighter but less substantial. I've never felt I could trust my guitar to one, but my doubts may be unfounded as ABS is extremely strong and a little lighter.

Microclimates

One bonus feature of a good case is that it creates a microclimate around your guitar. This is great when extremes of temperature and humidity are encountered – which doesn't just apply to desert travel and Arctic tours! At home in the winter, as humidity plummets, your case will provide a small volume of air that can be effectively temperature and humidity controlled. Consider installing a guitar humidifier if you live in a very dry area or are often surrounded by central heating.

Getting the 'right' sound

Musicians often come to the electric guitar having been inspired by a specific guitarist's 'sound'. In my case it was the magic of Hank Marvin. His clean and echo-delayed sound originated from a 1958 Fiesta red Stratocaster, plugged into a Meazzi Echomatic Delay, a Vox AC15 valve amp, and lashings of reverb added by Norrie Paramor from Abbey Road's wonderful valve EMT echo plates.

I didn't know any of that at the time – I just loved the sound from my Dad's 45rpm record. When I received a cheap acoustic guitar as a Christmas present it didn't make that sound and I was very disappointed. I could see no connection between that sunburst piece of firewood and the sound that I heard in my head.

It took me many years to 'join up the dots' and realise that both instruments shared the same tuning but were otherwise wholly different.

You may have come to the electric guitar inspired by Carlos Santana, Joe Satriani, Joe Perry, Jimi Hendrix or any of a hundred other players – and they all sound distinctly different. Each player has a 'voice'. That's one of the guitar's delights.

Some of that voice is about the individual and will never be matched, but other aspects of their 'sound world' can be attained; and finding that sound early on in your development as a player is a great motivator.

To start with you need to buy the right guitar. See the early part of this manual for guidance and seek out details of your favourite player's instrument. These days affordable versions are available of most classic guitars.

The amp is the next most crucial factor. I don't know any professional guitarist that uses a transistor or IC chip 'emulator' amplifier – they don't match the guitars' analogue output and usually sound plain wrong! Get a small valve amp and enter the real world. These are no longer prohibitively expensive. The modern electric guitar was designed in the 1950s to work with the quirky response of old-fashioned valves – and it does!

Then there's the FX. A bald electric guitar plugged straight into an amp rarely sounds entirely convincing, the exceptions being a huge

stadium, where it's immediately 'treated' by the room reverb and delay, and the studio, where again it's immediately compressed, EQ'd and delayed and reverberated, to produce the sounds we all know and love. So I suggest that very early on you explore the electric guitar's tonal palette via simple and affordable FX – even on your first chord, and certainly when you know three.

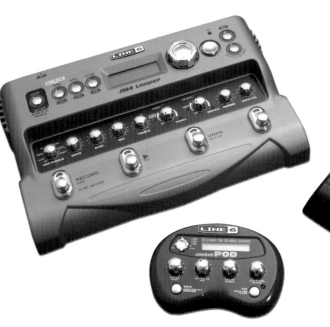

■ Chorus, phasing and flanging
Our ears and brains love the 'mind games' of shifting phase, messing with the time of arrival of a sound and possibly modulating the pitch at the same time – hours of fun for all guitarists. Think Badge from Cream, or any track from Police.

■ Tremolo
A gain modulation effect – throbbing pulsing and antique. Think Hey Bo Diddley.

The available options
By the time this book is published there will be new models of all these specific devices, but the principles have remained the same for the last 60 years – they just get better and cheaper! Digital Multi FX are the best value, though individual analogue devices have character and lots of fans.

■ Reverb
Reverberation isn't an artificial effect: the real world is full of reverb – the bigger the space, the more of it there is, from a bathroom to the Taj Mahal. Our ears love reverb and ideally your amp will have some on offer. If not, then consider an outboard device. For extreme examples think The Shadows and The Ventures, or any track from Phil Spector or Pink Floyd. Modern digital reverb is very versatile and affordable.

■ Wah wah
Changing your tone rhythmically and very swiftly with a foot pedal – think Voodoo Chile by Jimi Hendrix. Multi-FX units enable you to programme the same pedal to provide foot-controlled volume or 'swell'. Think Jimmy Page.

■ Delay
Delay is also a natural effect – we unconsciously use delay all the time to figure out where we are (aided by echoes from walls and floors), and it enhances all kinds of music. Digital delay devices offer everything from antique 'slapback' tape echo simulations to the Grand Canyon. Think Brian May – a master of the timed delay.

■ EQ
Think sophisticated tone controls – a huge range of 'colours' suitable for matching any tune. An undervalued 'effect' but crucial to finding a slot in the mix of any band.

■ Overload distortion
One of the reasons so many guitarists use valve amps is that they don't just amplify the guitar, they also enhance the sound with a rich palette of compression and harmonics. The more you turn up the gain/drive the more you get. A 'master volume' control means this need not be deafeningly loud. If you want more distortion this is now available in 50 different flavours. Think Slash and Jimi Hendrix.

■ A drum machine
In the 19th century we had a metronome – a bit boring, but it provided a steady pulse. Today some multi-FXs offer quite sophisticated looped drum samples, and playing along with these will improve every aspect of your timing and phrasing. This budget box even has an onboard tuner!

Remember, the guitar is the most versatile musical instrument ever created, so experiment, and have fun finding your sound.

A little light relic work

In rock legend the fashion for relic guitars started with the Rolling Stones' Keith Richards, who on receiving a new Telecaster told the Fender Custom Shop he would prefer it 'beat up a little'. Richards denies the legend, but the fashion is gaining momentum, with the Fender and Gibson custom shops offering 'Relics' in varying degrees of distress, from 'New Old Stock' to 'Heavy Relic' – all at a premium.

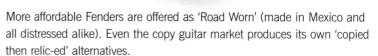

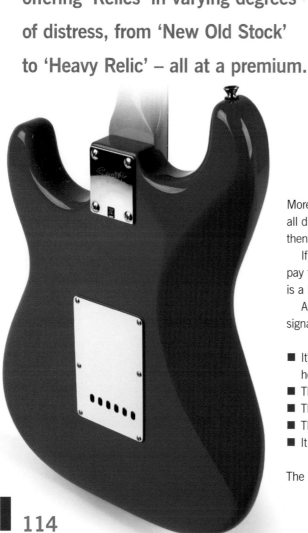

More affordable Fenders are offered as 'Road Worn' (made in Mexico and all distressed alike). Even the copy guitar market produces its own 'copied then relic-ed' alternatives.

If you prefer your guitars to look and feel 'played in' but don't want to pay for the privilege then you may consider a little DIY. All that's required is a little speeded up distress – doing 40 years of wear and tear in a day.

As an example I've chosen to gently distress a recent Biffy Clyro Squier signature Strat. The advantages of this model include:

- It's the right shape and approximate colour for the '62-era Strat he's often seen playing
- The headstock is the right shape and size.
- The bridge is a vintage six-screw type.
- The plastics come ready aged (in colour at least).
- It has a 'period correct' rosewood board.

The Squier arrived in the workshop looking pretty good but surreally shiny!

Proposed work

I thought I would demonstrate a few distressing techniques and leave it for you to decide the extent of distress you prefer.

The relic/antiquing process is necessarily different for contrasting components: wood requires abrasion and physical distress; metal requires simulated corrosion; fingerboards require very specific localised abrasion to simulate a played in feel; and plastic discolouration is an art in itself – so I'm going to cheat and use the 'aged' plastics readily available on this budget guitar and from many parts suppliers, and add a bit of graphite 'dirt' for the sake of authenticity.

However, if you feel you want to work on your existing parts these are some of the substances known to be used for plastic discolouration:

- A scotch pad or nail buffer.
- Kiwi brown shoe polish.
- Leather dye.
- Ritz clothing dye – yellow and sunset orange.
- A dirty hard rug.
- Incense.
- Cigarette smoke.
- Beer.
- Tabasco sauce.
- Wet coffee grounds.
- Tea.
- Evergreen stamping ink.
- Amber lacquer.
- 'Touch up' cabinet sticks.

These all have varied effects and permanencies. It's amusing sometimes when the ageing wears off some relics and reveals pristine white plastic!

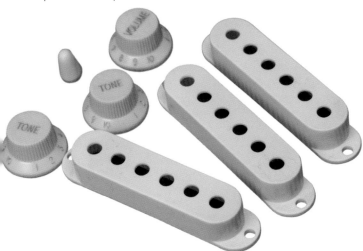

1 First disassemble the guitar – an electric screwdriver saves a lot of time.

2 A gentle waggle is good for removing tuner bushings.

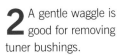

3 Keep a note of what goes where – a series of small resealable containers can be useful.

4 Keep a careful note of any neck pocket shims.

5 Carefully unsolder the jack socket and trem claw connections.

The bodywork

The body on this guitar is heavily coated with polyester, which by design is very resistant to extremes of temperature and will also take a lot of knocks and bangs. A real '62-era Strat would be finished in a far less durable nitro cellulose – the ageing effects here might include shrinkage and cracking, which are hard to simulate. I left this body out in the snow at –8° overnight and returned it to the drying cupboard three times – to absolutely zero effect!

1 However, losing the 'factory new' shine was easily achieved by a little light abrasion. I dipped a 1200 grit 'wet and dry' in a little white spirit to avoid clogging the paper and used a circular motion to lightly matt the surface. Screwing an old trem cavity cover and scratchplate in place means the 'ageing' effects will authentically only take place on the exposed parts of the body.

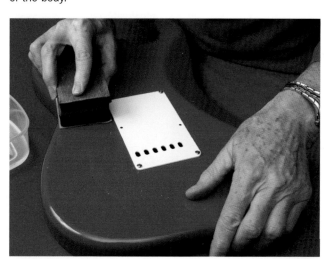

2 A little 0000-grade wire wool helps when addressing the more awkward corners and curves.

3 The removed trem cover shows the apparently 'oxidised' pattern.

4 The severe 'wear' pattern at the top bout was achieved with 320 grit freecut paper and a little more elbow grease.

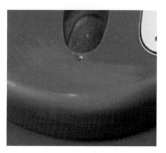

5 A similar wear mark near the jack plate could be elaborated with a few stage scars and dings.

A little 'dirt' simulation achieved by rubbing in some graphite dust will give a more believably aged appearance. The dings will be applied naturally and slowly by some regular gigging. This should put the dings in the correct places – guitar stand abrasion etc.

Oxidising the metal parts

On luthier John Diggins' recommendation I decided the safest approach to a metal 'oxidisation' effect was to use ferric chloride solution. This is readily available over the counter from 'Radio Shack'-type retail electronics outlets and is sold as Universal PCB Developer. The liquid is corrosive, but controllable and safe if you take a few simple precautions:

- Keep out of reach of children and animals.
- Ensure adequate ventilation and avoid inhaling any fumes.
- In case of contact with the eyes, apply liberal amounts of water and seek immediate medical assistance.
- After skin contact wash immediately with plenty of water.
- Wear overalls, gloves and eye protection.

Separate out the parts for ageing. Generally if a part has a direct mechanical function – such as a cog or bearing – leave it untreated, as you don't want to introduce any malfunctions, however authentic. Avoid threads and springs as far as possible.

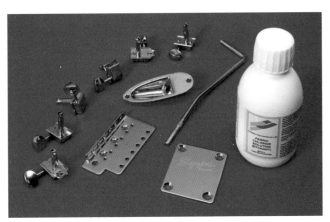

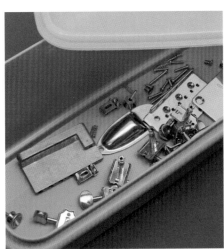

1 Lightly scratch the selected metal parts by putting them all together in a Tupperware box and using the box for a little Samba percussion workshop (shake 'em up!).

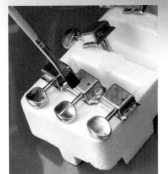

2 The brighter chrome parts will need a little direct abrasion with a paintwork abrasion pad and a little wire wool on the trem arm.

3 Then apply a little neat ferric chloride solution with a small brush and leave the parts to 'corrode' for 20 minutes.

4 Pushing all the screw threads into a polystyrene block means only the heads get the ageing treatment – authentic and desirable.

5 The tuners are only surface aged and still work perfectly.

6 The same applies to the other parts.

7 All the parts are then carefully rinsed in clean water to halt the corrosion process. Take care not to immerse the tuners!

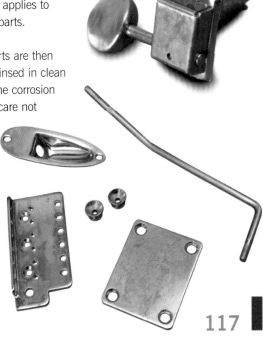

The neck

Even more so than the body, this is very glossy and looks a little unreal.

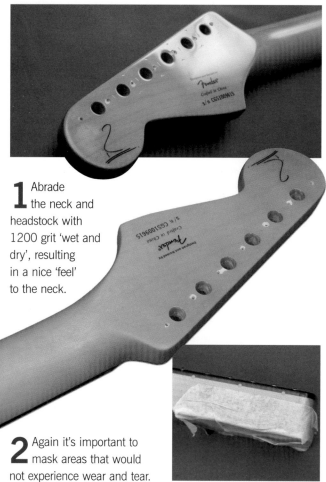

1 Abrade the neck and headstock with 1200 grit 'wet and dry', resulting in a nice 'feel' to the neck.

4 Sometime in a mythical '70s I let Eric Clapton play this guitar and he left his ciggie in the strings! Or was it a soldering iron?

2 Again it's important to mask areas that would not experience wear and tear.

5 I rolled the edges of the fingerboard with a medium grit file to get the 'played in' feel of Eric's 'Blackie'.

3 I was also careful not to remove the transfers, as I'm not pretending this is a Fender – it's clearly a Squier and has that brand's useful headstock truss rod access.

6 This needed a finish with a little 320 and 1200 grit paper.

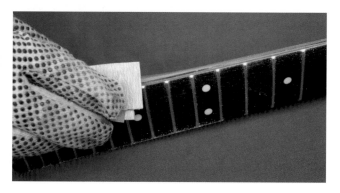

The plastic parts

As I said before I, chose this guitar as the plastic parts are already 'green mint' as supplied. You can buy 'mint' coloured parts from any number of websites, or for a DIY approach you could try some of the solutions suggested above. However, plastics age in subtle ways and I doubt if you could better the custom-coloured proprietary parts that are available.

What is needed is some abrasion – the new 'old parts' are very shiny and straight out of the mould.

1 The pickups are disassembled with a No '1' Phillips.

2 The pickups are bagged up and sealed to avoid them getting covered in iron filings, then the scratchplate is abraded with a players' plectrum pattern.

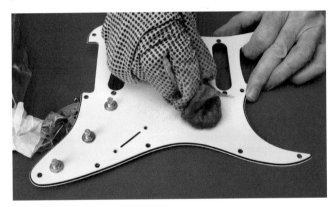

3 The knobs and pickup covers were also lightly abraded with some wire wool – they need a bit of muck in the serrated edges. Again I tried to abrade the pickup covers only where they surface. A little graphite from a pencil rubbed into the 'pick scratches' gives that ingrained dirt look.

4 The pickup pole piece tops were given a light rust treatment with a dab of ferric chloride and rinsed fairly quickly.

If you really want to go to town you could replace the plastic wiring with some period correct cloth-covered 'push back' wire and the small pots with some CTS full-size types etc – it's up to you.

The biggest giveaway in terms of period is the headstock truss rod access, but I suppose you could go mad and buy a '62-style neck! I will settle for changing the skinny alloy trem block for a brass replacement from Guitar Fetish (see page 120). This will improve the acoustic sound of the guitar, which always improves the amplified sound. The guitar also needed a new nut – the brittle plastic one supplied was, unusually, set too low. I'm building a bone nut from an oversize blank. See page 44 for more on nut work.

The finished 'light relic' looks pretty cool and a lot more appealing than an over-shiny Squier. The usual set-up procedures ensure that it plays damn good too!

Replacing an 'S'-type trem block

One of the saddest economies on cheaper 'S' types is their lightweight and skinny alloy trem blocks. These are detrimental to the sustain and stability of the trem, but are easily upgraded.

However, first check the position of the trem arm cavity on yours and the proposed replacement block – this can be a few millimetres 'off position' on some new blocks and makes a lot of work out of a potentially simple job. The new and old blocks need to have the same cavity positions or you may need to replace the whole trem assembly!

1 Remove the strings in the usual sequence of sixth/first, fifth/second etc. Then remove the rear trem access hatch with a No '1' Phillips screwdriver.

2 Remove the rear trem springs.

5 Move the saddles aside with a No '1' Phillips and replace the block, also using a No '1'. I had to remove three of the saddles to access the retaining bolts.

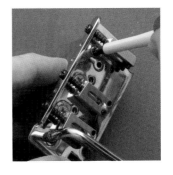

6 The new block is a substantial brass type from guitarfetish.com. It's important to check that the replacement doesn't touch the sides of the cavity.

7 Refit the saddles and realign. They will naturally need fine-tuning once the guitar is restrung.

3 Unscrew the bridge retaining screws, using in this case a 4mm screwdriver.

4 Make a note of the saddle positions as these will have to move to access the block retaining screws.

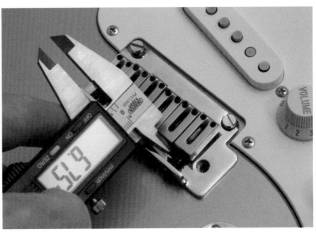

8 Reinstate the springs in the trem cavity.

9 Reassemble, restring and reintonate. Even played acoustically the resulting improvement in tone and sustain on this cheap Squier is startling. A mere $20 well spent (see 'Useful contacts and suppliers' appendix).

A patch repair on electric guitar bodywork

This Epiphone Les Paul is in 'as new' condition apart from one major ding on the rear top bout. It seems a pity not to fix this, especially as I prefer my guitars to look good. The urethane has simply flaked due to an impact of some kind and fortunately I taped the flake in position as soon as I came off stage.

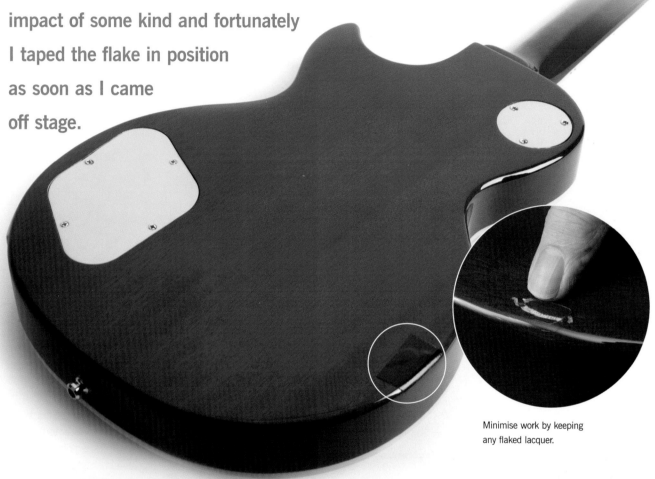

Minimise work by keeping any flaked lacquer.

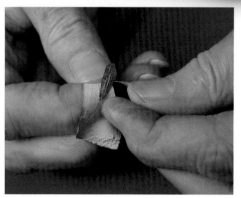

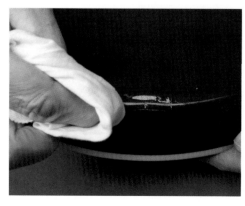

1 Removing the gaffer tape 12 months later the flake is still in place and luthier John Diggins suggested I glue the flake back and tidy up around it.

2 Clean off the adhesive tape residue with some white spirit, avoiding the bare wood (white spirit might inhibit the glue).

3 I then applied some superglue on a cocktail stick, for minimal glue damage to the surviving finish.

4 I then held the flake in place until the glue set, using a small plastic bag to prevent the fragment sticking to my fingers.

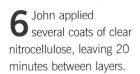

6 John applied several coats of clear nitrocellulose, leaving 20 minutes between layers.

7 Once the nitro was dry John carefully tinted the edges of the flake join with a little stained nitrocellulose...

5 I teased a little more glue under the edge of the join, then rubbed the surface smooth with some 320 and 1200 grit 'wet and dry'.

8 ...and then applied some more clear lacquer. This was left to harden for three days before using some T-Cut motor colour restorer to tidy up the finish and any slight overspray.

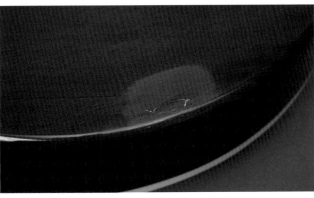

9 The finished repair is polished, rendering the 'ding' almost invisible.

All the spraying was done in a well-ventilated and dust-free environment with suitable extractor fans. Don't mess with nitrocellulose without taking proper precautions and wearing a mask and eye protection.

Specific case studies

There has never been a better time to buy an electric guitar, the present range, quality and variety being unsurpassed. The American makers offer superb homebuilt reissues of all their classics, and license affordable equivalents by Far Eastern manufacturers.

This means you could start with a classic 'S', 'T', 'SG' or 'LP' type and progress very quickly to 'a second guitar' of a retro or specialist type – a semi-acoustic or big-bodied 'Jazz box', a Danelectro or an Airline.

With a little work all these guitars can be made into giggable, reliable instruments that play well and sound great. Enjoy!

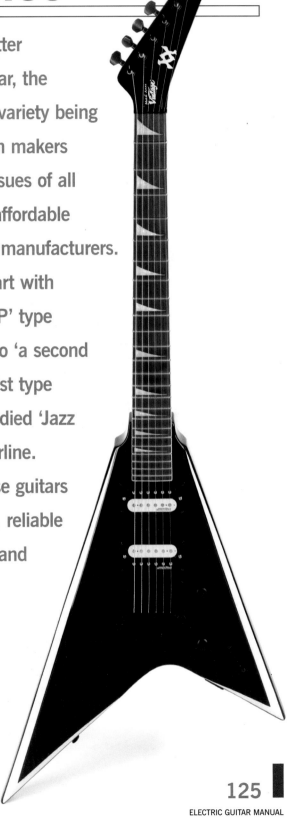

LEFT Our 'case study' guitars.

RIGHT An affordable 'Flying V'.

A classic 'S' type:
Squier Affinity series 'Strat'

The most popular electric guitar in the world and made under licence for Fender. A great classic design that just needs a thorough set-up. This particular guitar completed manufacture in Indonesia on 5 October 2009.

Made in Indonesia

Serial No.
ICS09108684

Getting up and running

The guitar arrives with a small transistor amp worth about $75, so that solves a common beginners' problem – the realisation that electric guitars don't really function on their own. The kit also includes plectrums, a gigbag, headphones, tuner, guitar lead, guitar strap, two Allen keys, a spare spring for the trem and a 'Getting Started' DVD – a very impressive package that potentially saves you about £50 ($75).

However, don't leave the shop or website without buying a decent set of strings – even if the fitted ones have survived the trip from Indonesia they'll be cheap and will have settled into the shape of the nut and saddles, which both currently need work. Also buy a 9V PP3 battery for the tuner! (For the record, the economy guitar tuner is a little flimsy and I had to solder one of the battery leads back on before we could get started!)

Condition on arrival

As is usual with Fender (and many other makes) this 'starter pack' guitar arrived 'shop ready', bedecked with an advertising sticker and a protective plastic coating on the scratchplate. The nut is very poor, overly high and badly cut from cheap soft plastic, and the trem isn't working! The pickups work, but are very prone to interference when not set to humbucking positions two and three. The guitar is great value and full of potential but is not quite yet a working musical instrument.

General description

■ Superficially this Indonesian 'Strat' bears a close 'Affinity' to the 1957 Vintage Stratocaster. To the casual viewer there is little significant visual difference. The pickguard is single-ply plastic with 11 Phillips No '1' screws. The tremolo arm, however, has a 1mm thread on a 5mm shank.

■ The body contours are of the generous vintage 'deep' type. This stems from Leo's original consultations with Bill Carson and other early Fender players, who often complained that the Telecaster slab body could dig into your ribs.

■ However, the body is usefully lighter, especially for a young beginner, with an overall guitar weight of about 7.5lb compared to a typical 8.25lb for a Vintage reissue. The body is also slightly thinner at approximately 1.6in, compared with the classic 1.75in. The guitar is made of alder/agathis laminate, which is an interesting reversion after many years of using pure economy agathis. This has a heavy coat of polyurethane, not traditional nitrocellulose.

■ The neck profile follows a usable half-round pattern and the headstock has a late '60s/early '70s vibe – large with recessed and exposed truss rod access.

■ The machine heads are of the bolt-on Fender/Gotoh type.

■ There are two string trees for the first to fourth strings, of the 'seagull wing' type.

■ Unlike a 1957 guitar the fingerboard is a slab of dark hardwood with a rosewood-like grain and has 'mother of plastic' dot markers.

■ The effective string headstock pitch is approximately 12°.

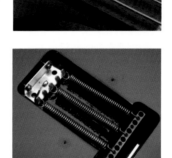

■ Surprisingly there is a 'skunk stripe' at the back of the neck even though the truss rod has been inserted before the fingerboard. The fingerboard has a modern 'American Series' radius of 9.5in.

■ The nut is soft white plastic and badly needs replacing, as the string spacing is way off and the tone is muted. See page 44 for more on sorting the nut.

■ The bridge is a cast saddle type but with the traditional six No '1' Phillips pivot screws, and requires a 1.5mm Allen wrench for adjusting the height and radius and a No '1' Phillips for intonation setting.

■ The trem/vibrato is also of the vintage type and has three of the five traditional balance springs. It also has two significant differences, which may affect the guitar's sound: the body routing is more extensive and deeper than a Vintage reissue (significantly more wood has been removed), and the trem block has substantially less mass (it is much thinner and made from a light alloy). Also there is no traditional spring in the trem cavity to retain the arm position. However, at present the thread is self-tightening.

■ The trem badly needs a set-up – it is bolted down, which is good for early tuning issues but a disappointment if you bought a Strat because it has one! See page 48 for set-up guidance. The trem arm thread is a 25G, should you need a replacement.

■ The guitar comes supplied with Fender 3250 009-042 'bullet' strings. These provide a cosy fit for the strings in the trem block, which may help tuning stability.

Specific routine maintenance

Check the neck relief (see page 41). If the truss rod needs adjustment you'll need a 4mm Allen wrench.

When you're next changing strings it's worth checking the machine-head locking nuts, which tend to work loose. On the Squier this requires a 10mm socket spanner. Do not over-tighten them – just enough to stop the machine head moving in normal use.

At the same time check the string trees. The No '0' Phillips screws here also tend to work loose, which can affect tuning stability especially when using the trem/vibrato. Lubricating the tree grooves with a little Planet Waves' Lubrikit also prevents sticking. This may be easier done by removing the tree and applying some lubricant with a cocktail stick.

The rosewood-type fingerboard tends to dry out and will benefit from a little lemon oil.

If the frets seem a little unfinished – which is normal on an economy guitar – take the opportunity to polish these with some very fine abrasive paper. To do this mask the fretboard with a propriety fret mask, masking tape or a Stewmac fret guard. The fret masks save a lot of time if you're busy. This guitar needs a standard Fender 25.5in size.

The strap buttons come loose with use so give them a tighten and if necessary plug a loose hole with a cocktail stick and some superglue.

Tech Tip

Sometimes you get trouble with the factory-fitted Fender 'bullet' strings jamming in the trem block. These can be released by gently tapping on a small Allen key inserted from the top of the guitar (through the saddle).

Andy Gibson

Whilst you have the tools out it's worth tightening the output jack retainer. This tends to work loose, causing crackles and intermittent output. Tightening entails removing the recessed jack socket using a No '1' Phillips and getting a grip on the jack retainer itself with an open spanner as you tighten the front nut with an 11mm socket spanner. If you try and tighten from the exterior alone the socket will often turn and break the output wire solder, cutting off the guitar's output.

Setting string heights and intonation

The Affinity has a vintage-type bridge arrangement but with cast saddles as opposed to the classic pressed steel.

The Allen key adjustment requires a 1.5mm key and the intonation a No '1' Phillips. For a set-up follow the Fender-type bridge set-up on page 58.

Under the hood

As you might expect with a budget guitar, removing the pickguard using a No '1' Phillips screwdriver reveals a large two-humbucker cavity that's not quite a swimming pool. These large cavities will have some impact on the acoustic sound of the guitar but make humbucker installation very simple. The white marks are simply excess buffing compound, easily removed.

■ The pickup cavity has a light dusting of black paint that looks like carbon-based screening, useful for reducing electrical interference. However, it's non-conductive and so purely decorative.

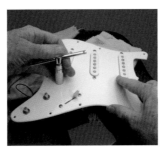

■ If loose the volume and tone pots require a 10mm socket spanner for removal or adjustment.

■ The tone pots are a tiny 'Alpha' 250K type common on economy Strats and these and the five-way selector have a minimal screening foil attached to the pickguard rear. A 2E223J capacitor (.022uF +/– 5%) bleeds high frequencies to ground via the two tone pots.

■ The five-pole switch is of a PCB type common on budget guitars. This would not be ideal for extensive professional use, but is adequate on what's intended as a student guitar.

■ The pickups are budget types with the effective magnetic pull coming not from the pole pieces themselves, which are quite weak, but from common bar magnets that sit across the back of these. The sound, however, is OK, with the familiar Strat snap.

■ The pickup height setting is held in place effectively, if a little crudely, by a couple of springs, and needs a No '1' Phillips for adjustment – best done with the strings on.

Signed off

The Affinity responded well to a general set-up. The truss rod had almost no tension as found – a couple of turns resulted in a flattish neck with the recommended relief. See page 41 for adjustment details.

The saddles were originally set too high with a random radius. This responded to the usual set-up as per a vintage 'S' type (see page 58).

The trem needed balancing but again responded easily to a typical vintage set-up (see page 48).

Overall the guitar did feel a little crude and slightly unfinished – the tremolo/vibrato in particular, despite a set-up, still seems unresponsive and dull, probably due to the much lower mass in the trem block. However, with a new set of strings the guitar plays almost as well as my Corona-made '57 reissue! This is remarkable for a budget instrument and a great testament to Leo Fender's original workmanlike plan.

Fender Frontman 15G amp

Supplied as part of the Squier 'starter pack' this 15W IC amp has the classic Fender look in a tiny affordable package – just £75 or so as a stand-alone purchase.

LEFT A tiny amp with lots of attitude.

General description

There are many small integrated circuit amps of this type out there. They solve the 'getting started' issue for beginners but can struggle to really deliver a convincing sound unless you're already a good player. However, that said this is one of the best small IC-based amps I've ever heard.

Specification

■ Inputs
One with two channels selected by a push button.

■ Auxiliary input
An extra RCA input for a CD/MP3 player, drum machine etc. This is really handy for rehearsing with a backing track. However, be aware that the playback device will need its own volume control, as the input is 'direct' to the output bus.

■ Headphone jack
The quarter-inch headphone jack is a protocol device for teenagers wanting to stay on good terms with their parents. The kit even comes supplied with headphones.

■ Channels
Two selectable channels (normal and drive). The two channels offer a straight clean sound and an overdriven sound, with control over the amount of overdrive.

■ Power handling
15W into 8 ohms – plenty enough for home rehearsal.

■ Controls
Normal volume, gain, drive select switch, drive volume, treble, mid, bass. The three-band EQ works very well.

Hardware

■ **Cabinet material**
Closed back cabinet.

■ **Handle**
Moulded black handle.

■ **Front panel**
'Blackface'-style control panel – a great classic Fender look.

■ **Amplifier dimensions**
Length 7.25in (18.41cm); width 13.25in (33.65cm); height 12.5in (31.8cm); weight 15lb (6.80kg).

■ **Effects**
None.

■ **Speaker**
1-8in Fender 'Special Design' speaker.

■ **Knobs**
Skirted amp knobs. IEC mains input (this is useful, as hard-wired mains leads are expensive to replace).

■ **Outputs**
Headphone jack.

BELOW A handy AUX input for MP3s.

Sound
The clean sound has a nicely compressed, distinctly Fender vibe. The overdrive sound is good for an IC design, albeit with the expected slightly synthetic quality when compared to a true valve response. Adding a simple FX unit provides reverb delay etc. To really get your show on the road see page 112 and get yourself into the right 'sound world'.

Upgrades
A version of this amp is available with reverb, but I would really advise moving up to a small inexpensive valve amp ASAP for authentic live guitar sounds. See page 176.

⚠ **Hazard Warning**

Do not venture inside guitar amplifiers unless you're qualified to do so, and even then be sure that the mains electricity has been disconnected.

A classic 'LP' type: Epiphone Les Paul Standard

Made in China

Serial No.
DW05110616

This guitar represents a typical example of the Epiphone 'Standard'. These now have a 'plus' top veneer featuring an attractive 'flame' effect. This particular guitar is finished in Cherry Sunburst, the original colour of what was in 1958 the Les Paul 'Regular'. Ironically the guitar is finished with modern urethane which will not fade to the coveted faded 'burst effect of the 1950s!

It has factory-fitted Epiphone USA-designed humbuckers with alnico magnets, which are double vacuum waxed with enamel wire. These sound pretty good but on page 102 we experiment with Seymour Duncan replacements – a common upgrade for this guitar.

General description

■ The volume and tone knobs are the vintage-type gold witches' hats, but moulded gold plastic, not 'back painted' as on the vintage guitars.

■ The three-way switch has an appropriate new minted appearance.

■ The pickup covers are chromium-plated, as are almost all the metal parts.

■ The fingerboard is raised bound rosewood.

Condition on arrival

The guitar is new and comes with a budget lead and an Allen key for the truss rod. The finish is dominated by a slightly garish red, very authentically rock'n'roll – my teenage pupils love it! The supplied flight case is a budget-conscious brown cardboard box.

■ At 7.75lb (3.5kg) the guitar is comfortably light for a Les Paul and may have some weight-reducing cavities. The body appears to be the vintage sandwich of maple and mahogany – however, the low weight points to alder with a thin veneer of mahogany and maple. The thick cherry-coloured finish cannot disguise the fact that the bottom 'mahogany' layer is in fact made up of at least three separate pieces of timber. This is no crime, especially in an economy guitar – we should remember that the first Goldtops often had three-piece carved tops. In the climate of the early 21st century recycling of what are probably offcuts is in fact a laudable endeavour. The laminate nature of all Les Pauls is in fact a major contributor to the guitar's famous rigidity – the 'railway track' principle Lester Polfus describes in his intro to my Les Paul book. Alder is a great tonewood that produces a brighter sound than mahogany.

■ The neck profile follows a typical slimmer, almost 1960 profile with a fairly constant depth. The neck seems one-piece and is too heavily stained for wood identification. It has a narrow '60s heel.

■ The bridge is of the Tune-O-Matic type with the usual thumb-screws for height adjustment and convenient Epiphone top screws – this bridge is on separate posts not set directly into the table.

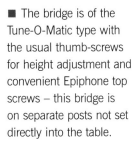

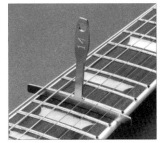

■ The string length adjustment requires a conventional straight-slot 4.5mm screwdriver accessed from the pickup side. The bridge has '50s-type metal saddles but with a 'modern' retaining spring.

■ The body is approximately 4.5cm thick at the edge binding and 5.5cm at the highest point of the top carving, slightly thinner than some vintage guitars. Some of the binding is a little low-budget. The apparent 'flamed' top is a very thin veneer, as is common on these budget guitars, but very convincing.

■ The fully bound fingerboard is of a dark rosewood with plastic trapezoid block inlays. The fingerboard radius is a 'blues friendly' 14in – unusual for a Les Paul, which is more often 12in.

■ The truss rod is accessed at the headstock, requiring a No '1' Phillips to remove the truss rod shield with it's distinctive 'Les Paul Standard' logo, and a 4mm Allen wrench for any adjustment. The frets are the 2.78mm/.109in gauge found on many later Les Pauls.

■ The supplied nut is a piece of plastic which needs some adjustment – see page 44 for a modification to bone.

■ The machine heads are good modern chrome Grovers with 'Ace of Clubs' tuning pegs.

■ The headstock has one of the distinctive Epiphone shapes first established in the 1930s.

■ The headstock angle is approximately 17°, unusual for an Epiphone but very welcome, giving a good downward pressure at the nut – important for tone and string stability.

Specific routine maintenance

First check the neck relief with your feeler gauges. The neck should be fairly flat – perhaps .015 relief at the 7th fret given .012in at the first fret first string. If the neck does need adjustment, the Standard requires the supplied 4mm wrench.

Follow the Tune-O-Matic set-up guide (page 64) for any bridge height and intonation adjustments.

A factor worth considering is the string angle between the Tune-O-Matic bridge and the stop tailpiece. Ideally this should be a steep slope to give a good string purchase at the bridge. However, at too steep an angle the strings can snag on the back of the Tune-O-Matic, which may cause premature string breakage as well as unpredictable string slippage. This specific guitar has been well set up with a good clearance.

The strings on this guitar are .010–.046, a common choice for this shorter scale guitar. When changing strings it's worth checking the machine-head fixing screws, which tend to work loose. This requires a No '1' Phillips. Do not over-tighten them – just enough to stop the machine head moving in normal use. The Grovers also have tension screws for the machine heads, which should be loosened for string changes using a No '1' Phillips and re-tensioned once the guitar is at pitch.

Whilst you have the tools out it's worth tightening the output jack retainer. This tends to work loose, causing crackles and intermittent output. Tightening entails removing the square plastic jack socket panel using a No '1' Phillips and getting a grip on the 12mm rear jack socket nut as you tighten the exterior nut with a 12mm socket spanner.

The scratchplate retaining bracket is best tightened OFF the guitar, as the rear nut is otherwise difficult to adjust without damage to the guitar top. Removing the scratchplate itself requires a No '1' Phillips screwdriver, and for tightening the rear retaining nut a 7mm socket spanner. Note how much better the guitar looks without the 'afterthought' scratchplate.

The strap-lock buttons are worth checking for secure fitting. If a No '1' Phillips screwdriver can't secure the screw then consider an improvised rawlplug made from a spent matchstick and a little superglue.

Under the hood

Removing the rear access panel using the usual No '1' Phillips screwdriver reveals a fairly clean rout, a little tatty around one of the pots, but the minimum of wood has been removed. During these inspections an aerosol lid can make a useful 'screw keep' avoiding accidental losses.

■ The wiring is competent, with four small modern 500K pots and .02mF capacitors routed to a three-way switch. All the wire is modern PVC-covered. The pots are roughly mounted to bare or painted wood and all the wiring is screened using an earthed loom. A nice touch is the modern wiring connector, which may make things easier and convenient should you wish to change pickups. The cream backing plates for the control cavities are a nice touch – a change from the traditional black.

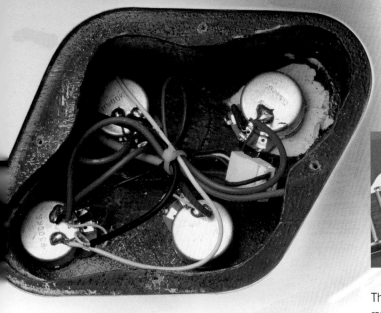

■ Revealed by removing the four Phillips No '1' screws, the Standard has USA-designed Epiphone humbucking pickups. These are designated '57 CH (G) Dot neck/bridge LP' and 'bridge HOTCH (G) BHC'.

'57' may refer to the PAF spec, and BH to 'burstbucker'. The pickups have been twice wax dipped – a measure which reduces any tendency to high frequency audio feedback. Access to the fragile coils is sensibly denied by a soldered seal.

Removing the metal 'cans' or cases is NOT recommended. Though this might look cool it exposes the pickups to environmental damage, will permit some induced hum, and will only make the pickups more treble-biased (due to stray capacitance). The sound of a Les Paul is a warmer sound best left alone. If you want the 'cool' bare pickup look this is easily achieved by buying a set of open case pickups from Seymour Duncan or similar.

■ If loose, the volume and tone pots require a wrapped-round duster to safely remove the push-fit knob and then an 11mm/ 0.5in socket spanner for removal or adjustment of the pot itself.

■ The three-way switch really needs a specialist tool for tightening and replacement – the plastic type protects the metal plating from damage.

■ If required, replacing the cheap but serviceable three-way switch is done via another rear panel. A modern 'rounded end' paperclip is a useful gizmo for removing these rear panels, as they're often a tight fit even when unscrewed. The rounded end avoids any potential scratching. All the panels are this complementary cream plastic with a textured finish.

■ The full-size Epiphone humbucker-type pickups in their custom cases require a No '1' Phillips screwdriver for adjusting their height in relation to the strings.

■ The overall pickup height adjustment is effected by two Phillips No '1' screws attached to a rear metal plate. 'Springing' is achieved by two substantial springs. The individual pickup pole adjustment requires a 4mm straight-slot screwdriver. When reseating humbuckers take care to ensure their correct orientation – in the case of the neck pickup this means putting the adjustable pole pieces nearest to the fingerboard.

■ The neck pickup cavity reveals the absence of the Les Paul signature 'long tenon'; on the 'full price' guitars this contributes to the strength of the neck join and the rigidity of the guitar – a factor in the Les Paul sound. Also revealed are some of the weight relief cavities often found on modern guitars, which are welcome in some ways but are also a factor in moving away from the classic Les Paul.

■ If for any reason you're removing all the strings then an elastic band prevents the loose stop bar falling off and doing damage.

Signed off

The Epiphone Standard required substantial setting up. Some of the frets were a little proud and the nut could be filed a little lower. Also, the Tune-O-Matic could come down a little – but this is all to be expected on a factory-finished economy guitar.

This is a lot of Les Paul for the money, and when wound up delivers something very like the classic 'burst sound. Some people have experienced problems with these guitars when wound up very loud, so please see page 102 for a suggested pickup swap.

A classic 'T' type:
Fender Squier '50s-vibe Telecaster

Made in China

Serial No.
CGSO80400833

The essence of the Tele type is simplicity of electrics combined with a strong bridge pickup – the heart of the 'T' type sound. This guitar features many of the characteristics of the classic original Fender design circa 1952, but at a very affordable price. The pine body is a reversion to Leo's early prototypes. Many regard this first solid-body electric production guitar as epitomising 'all you really need'.

General description

■ All the screws on this guitar are the modern Phillips type employed by Leo Fender from 1952–53 as he realised the virtues of automobile assembly line practice.

■ The volume and tone knobs are similar to the vintage types found on '50s Fenders. These are knurled and have a flat top.

■ The three-way switch has the early '50s distinctive black rounded 'top hat' knob, a copy of the Harry Davies type. The three positions are a modern forward or 'neck' position, middle for both pickups, and 'back' position for the bridge pickup alone. The tone and volume pots remain in circuit in all positions.

Condition on arrival

This new guitar arrives in a no frills cardboard box with no accessories or case. It needs a set-up, as budget guitars inevitably do. Disappointingly the guitar has a slight acid burn on the chrome control plate. However, this is easily remedied these days as Fender-type parts are readily available for all the classic models. Suppliers Peter Cook's immediately supplied a replacement plate.

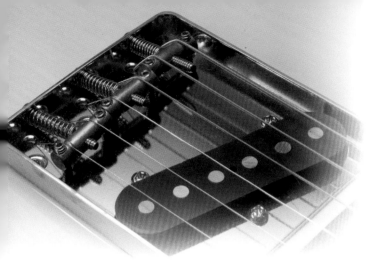

■ The custom Alnico III bridge pickup has the un-staggered pre-'52 pole pieces designed to replicate that eccentric unbalanced output from the six strings.

■ The traditional look Alnico I neck pickup has six separate poles beneath the stray-capacitance absorbing chrome cover.

■ The bridge, with its 'two strings per saddle' adjustable for height and length and integral relationship with the pickup, is an important part of this guitar's sound, and many distinguished players including Jerry Donahue prefer this arrangement to a more modern 'one string per saddle' set-up (see 'Saddle up your Tele' on the internet for Jerry's solution).

■ This instrument has brass saddles, and in a nice compromise of the authentic design it comes *with* the six slots you need!

■ Originally all '50s and many '60s Teles had a chrome 'ashtray' cover over the bridge. This made good cosmetic and even electrical screening sense, but prevents the player from palm muting and 'playing on the bridge', both of which techniques are key to the classic Tele sound. Consequently most 'ashtrays' are 'missing in action'. This guitar is supplied sans 'ashtray', but they're readily available for an authentic sound and look. George Harrison, Jimmy Bryant and Albert Collins are among the players who retained the 'ashtray' intact.

■ The 'through-body' stringing is an important part of the early Fender guitar sound. Note the ferrules are flush as on the 1950 Nocaster, not proud as on the current American Standard.

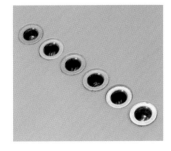

■ The pine body is fairly light for a two-pickup guitar at 7½lb and is approximately 1¾in thick at the edge. The guitar has a very thin white finish, designed to show off the grain.

■ The neck profile is a slim modern 'C' shape, with a fairly constant maximum depth of approximately ¾in. The back of the neck and the integral fingerboard have a gloss polyurethane finish.

■ The once innovative plain unbound fingerboard is of maple and the fingerboard radius is a modern 9½in, which is perfectly mirrored at the bridge. The frets are a medium 2.8mm gauge.

■ The truss rod is accessed practically in the 'modern' style at the headstock. Any adjustment requires a 5mm Allen or hex wrench. The 'Righty Tighty, Lefty Loosy' principle applies – go left a bit first to check for freedom of movement!

■ The nut is a piece of synthetic bone which is poorly cut. The strings are too high generally, but particularly on the treble side.

■ The machine heads are reproductions of the Kluson type Fender employed from mid-1951 and have no attribution.

■ The headstock echoes the distinctive early '50s shape and carries the Fender Squier logo. The double logo takes up a lot of space and consequently the '50s-type string tree is moved back much further than is ideal. The tree echoes the original improvised ferrule made from a nut and some washers – a very Leo Fender engineering solution.

Specific routine maintenance

First check the neck relief with your feeler gauges. The neck should be fairly flat – perhaps .015 relief at the seventh fret given .012in at the first fret first string. If the neck does need adjustment, the guitar requires a 5mm Allen or hex in the 'modern' headstock access hole.

Follow the 'S' and 'T'-type set-up guide (page 58) for any bridge height and intonation adjustments (you'll need a 1.5mm Allen or hex for the height adjustment). When adjusting the length of the string travel for intonation the spring may not always actually move the saddle – it will be inhibited by string pressure – so remember to reset the saddle with a screwdriver as a lever; it may not move otherwise. The string length adjustment requires a No '2' Phillips screwdriver.

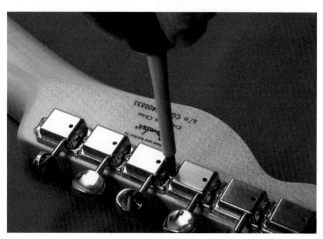

The 'top hat' knob is inclined to fall off, but using a little PTFE tape to thicken the thin post will prevent a common loss.

At .009–.044 the strings on this guitar are lighter than any commercially available in 1952. These are, however, consistent with Nashville stringing, *ie* employing a banjo string for a first and using the normal guitar first as a second and so on – a '50s solution to a craving for pliable guitar strings before the invention of light gauge 'Fender Rock'n'Roll'. James Burton first used this solution on his Tele in '58 on Ricky Nelson's *Believe What You Say*.

When changing strings, it's worth checking the machine-head fixing screws, which tend to work loose. This requires a No '1' Phillips screwdriver. Do not over-tighten them – just enough to stop the machine head moving in normal use.

Whilst you have the tools out it's also worth tightening the infamous output jack retainer. This early countersunk design tends to work loose, causing crackles and intermittent output. Tightening entails removing the chromed jack socket fitment and getting a grip on the jack socket itself as you tighten the exterior nut with a ½in socket spanner. In this particular case the chromed milled fitment was actually very secure and a quick tighten of the 12mm nut was all that was required. Otherwise leave well alone – if it ain't broke, don't fix it!

The strap 'buttons' are worth checking for secure fitting. If a No '1' Phillips screwdriver can't secure the screw then consider an improvised rawlplug made from a spent matchstick and a little superglue.

The frets are fairly unfinished. A polish with a simple cardboard template and some light abrasive such as 'Planet Waves' fret polishing paper will make for smoother string bends. Wire wool will also do the job, but take care to protect your hands and eyes. The neck bolts sometimes require a little tightening with a No '2' Phillips screwdriver.

Under the hood

Removing the traditional (but nicely bevelled!) five-screw scratchplate using a No '1' Phillips screwdriver reveals a clean rout which is humbucker-ready should you wish to go the Albert Collins/Keith Richards route. Note also the minimal screening on the back of the scratchplate.

During these inspections an Asian food or canapés tray can make a useful 'screw and tool keep', avoiding accidental losses.

■ The wiring is a simple vintage arrangement but with modern 'economy' components – two small 250K pots and one .05mF capacitor wired to the three-way switch. All the wiring is modern plastic covered.

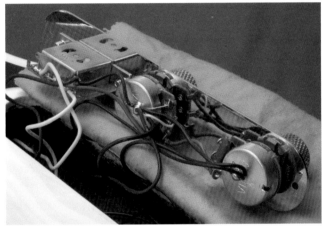

■ For the best tone and intonation be sure the bridge plate is well secured using a No '2' Phillips.

■ Removing the backplate with a No '2' Phillips reveals the pickup, which has the appearance of a classic early Tele with wax string protecting the fine over-wound coil. The pickup is designated 'TCA2B (Fender)-BK'.

■ When removing a pickup a simple 'pencil line on a business card' template takes the guesswork out of getting the original height on replacement. This neck pickup is also a sophisticated six-pole device with some height adjustment aided by an integral pad of soft foam rubber. Note the odd routing of the neck pocket.

■ If loose, the volume and tone knobs are a simple push-fit. An 11mm socket spanner is required for removal or adjustment of the pot itself.

■ The three-way switch needs a No '2' Phillips driver for tightening and replacement of its steel bolts.

■ The bridge pickup in its patented housing requires a No '1' Phillips screwdriver for adjusting its height in relation to the strings. Typically this has a three-point adjustment.

■ The neck pickup is designated TCA2N (Fender)-NK and sits on an unusual ½in thick black foam rubber pad. It has six separate pole pieces.

A classic semi-acoustic: Epiphone Dot 'Natural'

The semi-acoustic guitar has a distinctive sound of its own – a little hollow and 'woody'. This distinct voice has featured on everything, from the music of The Beatles and Brit pop band Oasis to the urban groove of Larry Carlton and the definitive blues of BB King.

Made in Korea
Serial No.
09121500739

Gibson realised early on that the downside to the ES330 semi was its tendency to acoustic feedback, and responded with the classic Gibson 'Dot' ES335 of 1958–62. This version of the semi is in fact almost solid, with a centre block of timber significantly supporting the pickups and diminishing the hollow cavities that increase the likelihood of resonant acoustic feedback. The Epiphone Dot is a great practical starting point for those aspiring to a semi sound. It has the cool look of a Beatles/Oasis Epiphone Casino but also the rationalised humbuckers and solid build of the Gibson 335.

Getting up and running

First change the strings for some decent .009–.042 D'Addarios or similar, which will tune better and their light gauge will save you some strain on your unexercised digits! See page 36.

The guitar will definitely need a set-up in order to stay in tune and be easy to play – see pages 64. New strings are essential for a set-up as their intonation will be accurate.

Condition on arrival

This specific Dot combines the stripped look of a later period John Lennon Epiphone but with the practical specification of the Gibson 335. It belongs to guitarist Peter Holland of Corby. Peter also plays an excellent Gibson 'SG' and the Dot is his 'other' stage guitar, which he keeps in D tuning for specific songs.

General description

■ Superficially this Dot is a hybrid of the Epiphone Casino and the Gibson ES335. The name 'Dot' refers to the highly coveted first batch of Gibson ES335s, which featured dot-marker fingerboards rather than the block inlays associated with high-end Gibsons.

■ The 'long' pickguard coveted on original Gibson dots has the distinctive Epiphone 'e' badge (this one is removable, not integrated as on vintage Epiphones). The guard is held in place with two Phillips No '1' screws and a single bracket and nut and bolt (currently the wrong size!).

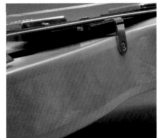

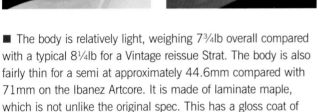

■ The body is relatively light, weighing 7¾lb overall compared with a typical 8¼lb for a Vintage reissue Strat. The body is also fairly thin for a semi at approximately 44.6mm compared with 71mm on the Ibanez Artcore. It is made of laminate maple, which is not unlike the original spec. This has a gloss coat of polyurethane, not traditional nitro cellulose.

■ The body has the expected internal 5in centre block running the length and depth of the body – an important aspect of the 335 Dot 'anti-feedback' design.

■ The three-piece mahogany neck has a profile bulkier than many 335s, which is a good thing for tone, and follows a usable half-round pattern. The headstock has a classic Epiphone profile of the 1960s and a 'Dot'-shielded truss rod access. The neck has a 24¾in scale length.

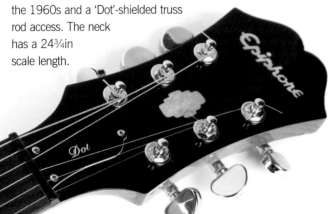

■ The machine heads are modern tensionable bolted Grovers, which on a working guitar is a sensible modernisation of the expected Klusons.

■ Like a 1958 model, the fingerboard is a slab of dark hardwood with a rosewood-like grain and has 'mother of plastic' dot markers.

■ The unbound fingerboard has a modern radius of 15in, which is almost matched at the bridge.

■ The headstock pitch is only 12°, much less than the classic 17° of pre-'66 Dots.

■ The nut is soft black plastic, with a width of 1.68in.

■ The bridge is an Epiphone Tune-O-Matic with two 5mm height bolts and six 4mm intonation bolts.

What to look for in a Thinline semi

For a working stage guitar, you really need a feedback-reducing centre block inside the hollow body and some PAF-like humbuckers or P90s. A good rigid set neck and a decent set of tuners make for a guitar that stays in tune.

141

Specific routine maintenance

Check the neck relief (see page 41). If the truss rod needs adjustment you'll need a 4mm Allen wrench. See page 41 for any adjustment.

When you're next changing strings it's worth checking the machine-head locking nuts, which tend to work loose. On the Dot this requires an 11mm socket spanner. The retaining screws require a No '1' Phillips. Do not over-tighten them – just enough to stop the machine head moving in normal use.

The guitar was supplied with .009–.046 strings.

Setting string heights and intonation

If you need to set the string heights and intonation, 'The Dot's' Tune-O-Matic type bridge arrangement is easier to adjust than a Gibson, as the height can be set with the top screws. For a set-up follow the Tune-O-Matic type bridge set-up on page 64.

An interesting and useful feature of these modern Epiphone stop-tails is the simple spring clip that prevents the stop-tail flying off and causing damage to the guitar.

The pickup height setting is held in place effectively, if a little crudely, by a couple of springs and needs a No '0' Phillips for adjustment. This is best done with the strings on. See page 86 for recommended pickup heights.

If the frets and fingerboard seem a little unfinished – which is common on an economy guitar – take the opportunity to polish these with some 000 grade wire wool. If the fingerboard is already smooth you could just polish the frets with some very fine abrasive paper. To do this, mask the fretboard with either a propriety fret mask, masking tape or a Stewmac fret guard. A fret mask will save a lot of time if

you're busy. This guitar needs the Gibson 24¾in size. (See Useful contacts appendix.)

The rosewood-type fingerboard tends to dry out anyway, but after a polish will benefit from cleaning with a little lemon oil.

The strap buttons work loose with use so give them a tighten with a No '2' Phillips and if necessary plug a loose hole with a cocktail stick and some superglue. This may save your guitar from a nasty plunge to earth, which often removes the headstock on these guitars.

Whilst you have the tools out it's worth tightening the output jack retainer. This tends to work loose, causing crackles and intermittent output. Tightening entails a 'Jack The Gripper' tool to keep the jack from revolving, and a 13mm socket spanner to tighten the nut. If you try and tighten from the exterior alone the socket will often turn

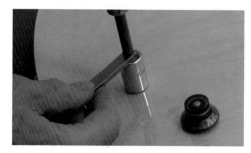

and break the output wire solder, cutting off the guitar's output. This is really difficult to fix on these guitars due to limited access.

Under the hood

■ The pickup cavity is cut into the centre block as if this were a solid electric guitar. The Alnico magnet pickups are '57 CH(G) BHC Epiphones. Both pickups appear to have the same spec.

■ The pickup cavities have a thin layer of carbon-based screening paint, which helps to reduce induced interference. However, this paint is not grounded to earth so is minimally effective.

■ If the volume and tone pots are loose the gold knob usually comes off with a duster. The nuts themselves require an 11mm socket spanner (wrench) for removal or adjustment.

■ The three-pole switch is of a type common on budget guitars. It would not be ideal for extensive professional use, but is adequate on what is intended as a student guitar. Tightening a loose switch requires a metric toggle switch wrench – this is made of plastic to avoid damaging the securing ring or the guitar body.

■ The tone and volume pots are 500K type common on humbucker-equipped guitars.

Signed off

The Dot responded well to a general set-up involving a fret polish, intonation set and some nut work. The neck was initially convex but this was eventually fixed by slowly releasing a little tension on the truss rod over 24 hours. See page 41 for truss rod adjustment details.

The basic sound has plenty of character and it would be worth installing some upmarket humbuckers at a later date to really get the most from this instrument. A four-wire humbucker would open up lots of authentic Varitone potential for BB King fans. A 'Lucille' version is actually available from Epiphone and is a very fine guitar – the example shown, owned by talented young guitarist Dan Cargill, has a microtune tailpiece as found on the original Gibson.

The guitar recently passed through the workshop, and required a little fretwork. It's shown with a Stewmac 'Epiphone pattern' self-adhesive fret mask, saving a lot of tedious masking.

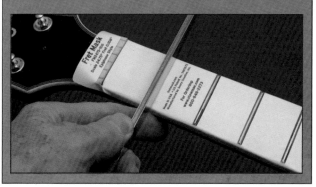

A jazz box with ambition: Ibanez Artcore AF75TDG-IV

We live in exciting times – who would have thought a 'White Falcon'-like guitar could be had for $400? So, if you fancy a little 'rockabilly' or Duane Eddy, this may be the guitar for you.

Made in China

Serial No.
S09033390

Getting up and running

This guitar arrives without an amp – bear in mind that a good amp is as important if not more important than the guitar! (See page 176.) Also, don't leave the shop or website without buying a decent set of strings. Even if the fitted ones have survived the trip from the other side of the world they'll be cheap and will have settled into the shape of the nut and saddles. Also buy a tuner and a good lead.

Change the strings for some appropriate D'Addarios, which will tune better and their lightish gauge will save you some strain on your unexercised digits! See page 36.

Ideally get a pro to adjust the nut, but if you're sufficiently keen to do it yourself see page 44.

The guitar will definitely need a set-up in order to stay in tune and be easy to play – see page 64. The importance of tuning and set-up are particularly crucial in the early stages of learning, so let nobody tell you otherwise; you'll just give up if you get too many calluses and the sodding thing still sounds bad! Never think 'It's OK for now' – the early stages of learning are the hardest and the most crucial, so you need a decent set-up right now.

Condition on arrival

The guitar arrived in good condition and set up well enough to go straight on stage. I recently played the Eddie Cochran tribute reissue guitar from Gretsch, and whilst that had all the expected mojo the Ibanez is actually a far better practical instrument for a modern gig. The optional AF100C case comes at about an extra hundred dollars, though Hiscox do a suitable alternative for less.

144

General description

■ The semi transparent volume and tone knobs are reminiscent of Gibson 'speedknobs' and operate in the familiar 'one tone one volume for each pickup' arrangement.

■ The Gibson style three-way switch is simple and effective, giving the expected neck/both/bridge combinations – though awkwardly positioned if you're also using the vibrato.

■ The pickup covers and all the metalwork are 'gold'-plated for lots of glamour.

■ The scratchplate is a floating cream-coloured plastic job, secured with two Phillips screws and a 'gold'-plated L bracket.

■ The Bigsby-style trem has a movable arm. The VBF70 Vintage Vibrato has one substantial motorcycle spring arranged in a conventional Bigsby-like housing.

■ The single cutaway is vintage style, which looks cool but means you have far less access to the dusty end of the fingerboard than you might expect.

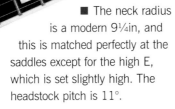

■ The neck radius is a modern 9¼in, and this is matched perfectly at the saddles except for the high E, which is set slightly high. The headstock pitch is 11°.

■ The bridge is an interesting hybrid incorporating a Tune-O-Matic top section with the expected intonation adjustment and height thumbwheels but with the addition of Gretsch-style floating rollers – ably assisting the strings to move in synch with the vibrato. The lower support section of the bridge is a more 1930s wooden platform.

■ The total body weight is a comfortable 7¼lb, slightly lighter than the average Strat. The body measures 40cm lower bout and 30cm upper bought, and the hollow body depth is approximately 7cm. The top, sides and back are all maple.

■ The neck profile follows a modern, slim 'U', tapering at the nut to just under 2cm. The neck is a heavily polyurethane-coated piece of mahogany with the frets bound into a rosewood fingerboard. There are block pearloid markers at frets 1, 3, 5, 7, 9, 12, 15, 17, 19 and 21, with 22 frets overall. The frets are medium 2.6mm gauge.

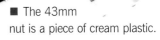

■ The 43mm nut is a piece of cream plastic.

What to look for in a Rockabilly guitar

Bling plays a part in the look of these guitars, as does the deep body; but if the bling is applied to a Bigsby-style trem and there are some Filtatron-like pickups then we're really ready to jive! For anyone with a hankering to twang, this guitar made in 2009 represents a vogue for retro styling and echoes the golden age of the Gretsch White Falcon. It has been built to closely resemble a similar guitar produced in the 1950s, but has an 'as new' finish.

Specific routine maintenance

First check the neck relief with your feeler gauges. The neck should be fairly flat – perhaps .010 relief at the seventh fret

sixth string with a capo at the first fret and the string stopped at the last fret. If the neck does need adjustment the Artcore requires a 4mm Allen wrench as shown above.

For any intonation adjustment the Artcore has a Tune-O-Matic arrangement. As the height affects the intonation it's important to get this right first, setting the two thumbwheels to your desired height and then adjusting the length of each string with a 5mm straight-slot screwdriver. If you're unsure how to do this see page 64, 'String height and intonation on a Tune-O-Matic type bridge'.

Lubricating the roller bridge with a little Planet Waves' Lubrikit will ensure a better return to pitch when using the vibrato.

The spring and all moving parts of the VBF70 will also benefit from light lubrication.

The strings on this guitar are .009s D'Addarios, though for an authentic '50s sound I'm going to try some .012–.052 Pro steels with a wound third – this may entail some adjustment of the truss rod and certainly the intonation. Be aware when removing all the strings on this type of guitar that the bridge is free-standing, so mark its position with a little low-adhesion tape to save a re-intonation, and also be careful that the 'free' bridge doesn't mark the guitar surface if it suddenly becomes too free!

When changing strings, it's worth checking the machine-head fixing screws, which tend to work loose. On the Artcore this requires a No '1' Phillips on the back and an 11mm socket wrench

on the front. Do not over-tighten them – just enough to stop the machine head moving in normal use. On this new guitar everything was loose.

Whilst the strings are off its worth giving the frets a polish. Having first masked off the fingerboard with some low-adhesion masking tape, I'm using some new 3M wet-and-dry flexible Polish paper 281Q (grade 3MIC) – this is micron-graded aluminium oxide on a non-woven synthetic backing – before finishing off with a strip of leather attached to a bit of scrap timber. Take care not to accidentally remove the nut!

I then finished the rosewood with the Dunlop two-pack cleaner.

The nut should be lubricated with a little graphite.

Whilst you have the tools out it's worth tightening the output jack retainer. This tends to work loose, causing crackles and intermittent output. Tightening entails putting a 'Jack The Gripper' in the socket and tightening the external nut with a 12mm socket spanner.

The three-way selector switch can be tightened with a 14mm socket wrench if the plastic knob tip is removed. Note the thumb through the F hole, keeping the switch from revolving.

Under the hood

Maintenance work isn't easy on any semi-acoustic but on this model the pickups are easily accessible and the Artcore also has usefully generous F holes.

Interior view.

■ The pickup height adjustment requires a No '1' Phillips screwdriver and the individual poles a 4mm straight-slot.

■ Removing the pickguard using the usual No '1' Phillips screwdriver gives better access to the pickups.

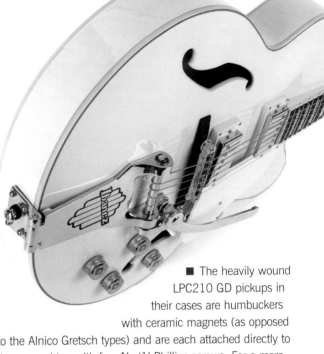

■ The heavily wound LPC210 GD pickups in their cases are humbuckers with ceramic magnets (as opposed to the Alnico Gretsch types) and are each attached directly to the pressed top with four No '1' Phillips screws. For a more authentic Gretsch sound TV Jones do an 'English' mount version of their TV classic which would drop straight in – see page 104.

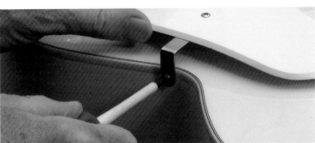

■ If loose the volume and tone pots require an 11mm socket spanner (wrench) for removal or adjustment. The knobs themselves are an easy push-fit.

■ Seen with an inspection mirror and interior light fed through the pickup cavities, the wiring is very neat with four tiny 500K pots and 0.1mFd capacitors routed via a modern three-way switch. All the wire seems to be modern PVC.

Signed off

This guitar is currently being gigged by the author's 'super hero alter ego' Frank Marvel. Marvel uses it as an affordable 'Gretschalike' for some late '50s early and '60s retro instrumentals, and it performs very well, though dodging acoustic feedback can be tricky!

With a decent set-up and these heavier strings the Artcore performs well. I suspect a switch to TV Jones 'Classics' will put the tone squarely in the right court.

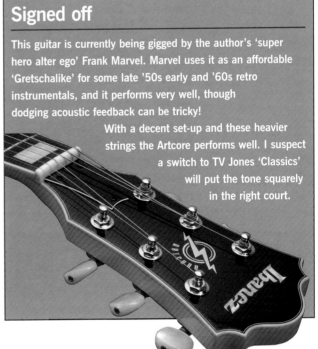

A classic retro guitar: Danelectro '63 DG 63 Aqua

Made in China

Serial No.
036319

These guitars were originally cheap alternatives for those players who couldn't afford a Fender or a Gibson. In the 21st century, they conjure up a little nostalgia and do have their own distinctive sound.

The Danelectro company was founded by Nathan Daniel in 1947. Throughout the late 1940s the company produced amplifiers for Sears, Roebuck and Company and Montgomery Ward, as well as, later, guitars for Silvertone and Airline. In 1963 an odd-looking guitar

burst on to the pages of the Sears catalog – Danelectro's 'Model 1449', which at $99.95 would soon become popular with garage bands. The Danelectro's pickups, ingeniously housed in real lipstick tubes, quickly

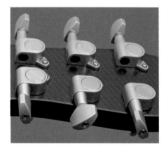

became known for their signature twang. The guitar bodies were lightweight and featured a hollow inner chamber that made them sonically more 'alive' than traditional solid bodies. They were often marketed under the Silvertone brand. Reissued versions of these guitars are now made by the Evets Corporation.

Getting up and running
On a practical front, you'll need a small valve amp (the originals had a 3W amp built into the case!), a guitar lead (it's worth shelling out for a good one), a decent set of strings, a tuner and a gig bag. See the chapters on Getting started and Getting your new guitar working properly for further guidance.

Condition on arrival
The guitar arrived in good condition and fairly playable, though it will benefit from some minor tweaks and a set-up.

General description

■ The total body weight is a very comfortable 6½lb – much lighter than the average 'S' type. This has no contours and is a fascinating amalgam of Masonite with a plywood core. There's also a lot of plywood from neck pocket to bridge, with hollow chambers to the sides and behind the bridge all contributing to a distinctive hollow sustain. The wallpaper tape vinyl binding completes the vintage vibe.

■ The two simple volume and tone knobs do the job and have authentic-looking 'radio shack' knobs. The three-way switch provides bridge, both and neck pickups in a clunky but working arrangement.

■ The pickup covers and all the metalwork are 'zero gloss' nickel-plated for period effect.

■ The scratchplate is a distinctive 'hole in the middle' in matt plastic, secured with five No '1' Phillips screws and based on the later 1457 model of 1964.

■ The double cutaways are vintage 'turned in' – 'Burns Bison' horn like – and give full access to the 19th fret.

■ The neck radius is a very modern fairly flat 15in, and this is reflected quite accurately at the saddles except for the low E, which is set slightly high.

■ The 'bottle style' headstock has an effective pitch at barely 10°. This is achieved with a thick fingerboard and high metal nut.

■ The back of the guitar has an access and hatch and four pickup retaining screws.

■ The strap buttons are nickel-coated types and require a No '1' Phillips.

■ The bridge is an interesting hybrid incorporating overall height adjustment on two simple screws and individual intonation adjustment accessed (with some difficulty) under the strings. It does work, but you don't want to be in a hurry! There's unfortunately very little pitch angle at the saddles – they're almost flat, in fact – though a centre screw offers some potential adjustment here (see below).

■ The bolt-on maple neck is painted satin black and the profile follows a '60s 'U' tapering at the nut to just under 2.3cm. The unbound frets are mounted in a rosewood fingerboard. There are simple plastic dot markers at frets 3, 5, 7, 9, 12, 15, 17 and 19. The frets are medium 2.8mm gauge and the scale length is 25in.

■ The machine heads are modern high-ratio tensionable types and require a No '1' Phillips at the back and an 11mm socket spanner at the front.

What to look for in a retro guitar

The retro appearance is as desirable as the distinctive sound of these unusual guitars. However, in today's gigging arena with higher audience expectations you also need a reliable instrument that will tune up and stay in tune and probably have a bit more output than the originals. This hybrid reissue addresses those challenges without too much obvious modernisation.

Specific routine maintenance

First check the neck relief with your feeler gauges. The neck should be fairly flat – perhaps .008 relief at the seventh fret sixth string with a capo at the first fret and the string stopped at the last fret. If the neck does need adjustment the Dano requires a 4mm Allen wrench as shown.

For any intonation adjustment the Dano has a hybrid arrangement. As the height affects the intonation it's important to get this right first – setting the two No '2' Phillips screws to your desired overall height. Fortunately there's also scope for improving the saddle break angle using a No '2' Phillips on the centre pivot screw; then the individual saddles may be adjusted to give the correct radius using a 1.5mm Allen key.

Then adjust the length of each string (intonation)

with a No '1' Phillips in a very crude 'jiggle'. If you're unsure how to do this see page 64 for details on setting up a Tune-O- Matic type bridge, as the principle is the same – if a little more awkward to adjust.

The strings on this guitar are anonymous .009–.042s, probably Dano's own brand.

When changing strings, it's worth checking the machine-head fixing screws, which tend to work loose. On the Dano this requires a No '0' Phillips on the back and an 11mm socket wrench on the front. Do not over-tighten them – just enough

to stop the machine head moving in normal use. On this new guitar half the screws were loose! This would naturally lead to tuning problems.

Whilst the strings are off it's worth giving the frets a polish. Having masked the fingerboard with some fret guards, I'm using some new 3M wet-and-dry flexible Polish paper 281Q (grade 3MIC) – micron-graded aluminium oxide on a non-woven synthetic backing – before finishing off with a strip of leather attached to a bit of scrap timber, which is easier done if the nut is unscrewed! An unusual option.

I then finished the rosewood with a little lemon oil.

The metal nut is a little high and needs some corrective filing and then lubricating with a little Lubrikit or Vaseline. The screw fixing mean there's no scope for filing the height of the nut from the bottom, so for filing the slots I'd suggest using some inexpensive needle files

NOT expensive nut files designed for working bone and plastics.

Whilst you have the tools out it's worth tightening the output jack retainer. This tends to work loose, causing crackles and intermittent output. Tightening entails putting a 'Jack The Gripper' in the socket and tightening the external nut with a 12mm socket spanner.

A loose three-way selector switch can be tightened with a 15mm wrench – some masking tape protects the matt pickguard from accidental scratches.

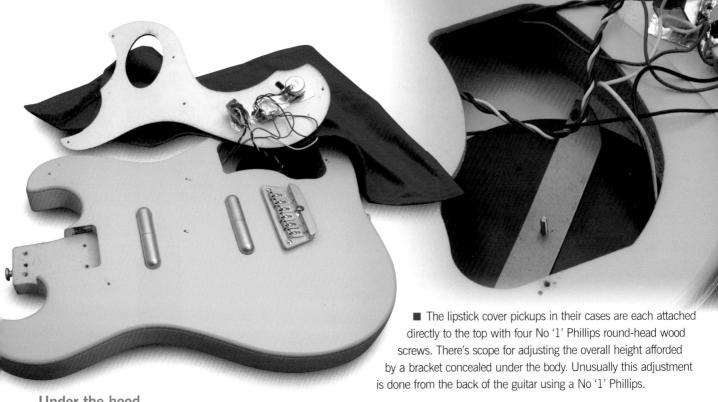

■ The lipstick cover pickups in their cases are each attached directly to the top with four No '1' Phillips round-head wood screws. There's scope for adjusting the overall height afforded by a bracket concealed under the body. Unusually this adjustment is done from the back of the guitar using a No '1' Phillips.

Under the hood

Removing the pickguard using the No '1' Phillips screwdriver shows the construction.

■ Removing the rear hatch with a No '1' Phillips reveals the extent of the body cavities – those are two 6in and 12in rulers disappearing! There are two substantial 500K pots and two capacitors (104J 100K and 2A102), routed via a modern three-way switch. All the wire is modern PVC. Replacing the cover requires care positioning the metal retaining bracket before tightening the central screw.

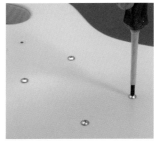

■ If loose the volume and tone pots require a 7/16in socket spanner (wrench) for removal or adjustment. The knobs themselves are an easy push-fit.

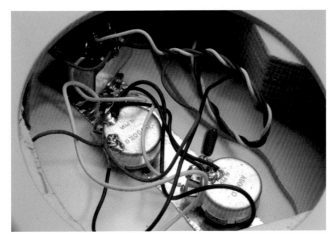

Signed off

This guitar looks like it sounds – a little quirky. Moving away from the sparkle of a Fender or the guts of a Gibson it cries out for first-position chiming chords with a charming 1960s innocence. It plays a lot better than the original cheap guitars of that era and could be used on stage. An expensive improvement on a cheap guitar with a lot of character.

Scale/length	635mm/25in
a	Width at nut 41.5mm
b	Width last fret 56.6mm
c	Thickness 1st fret 20.6mm
d	Thickness 12th fret 24.5mm

An economy 'Superstrat': Yamaha Pacifica 112V

The Pacifica has a well-deserved place as a favourite 'first guitar'. The combination of 'S' type styling and a humbucker at the bridge is very versatile and great value for money.

Made in Indonesia

Serial No.
not found

Getting up and running

A new set of strings, a fret polish and a little bridge and nut adjustment should get you on the road. If you need help with tuning and intonation see pages 58.

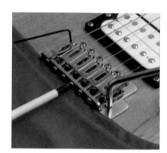

Condition on arrival

The instrument arrived in a simple cardboard box and covered in protective plastic film. This is best removed with the pickguard screws off. The set-up is workable if a little crude. The vibrato unit arrived set flat rather than 'floating' – this is a very stable intonation option for beginners, if a little boring and un-rock'n'roll.

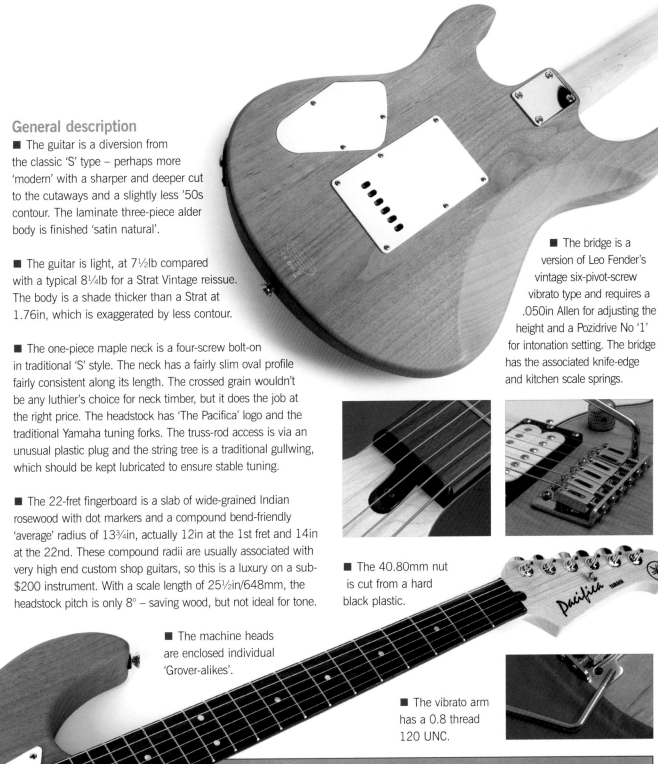

General description

■ The guitar is a diversion from the classic 'S' type – perhaps more 'modern' with a sharper and deeper cut to the cutaways and a slightly less '50s contour. The laminate three-piece alder body is finished 'satin natural'.

■ The guitar is light, at 7½lb compared with a typical 8¼lb for a Strat Vintage reissue. The body is a shade thicker than a Strat at 1.76in, which is exaggerated by less contour.

■ The one-piece maple neck is a four-screw bolt-on in traditional 'S' style. The neck has a fairly slim oval profile fairly consistent along its length. The crossed grain wouldn't be any luthier's choice for neck timber, but it does the job at the right price. The headstock has 'The Pacifica' logo and the traditional Yamaha tuning forks. The truss-rod access is via an unusual plastic plug and the string tree is a traditional gullwing, which should be kept lubricated to ensure stable tuning.

■ The 22-fret fingerboard is a slab of wide-grained Indian rosewood with dot markers and a compound bend-friendly 'average' radius of 13¾in, actually 12in at the 1st fret and 14in at the 22nd. These compound radii are usually associated with very high end custom shop guitars, so this is a luxury on a sub-$200 instrument. With a scale length of 25½in/648mm, the headstock pitch is only 8° – saving wood, but not ideal for tone.

■ The bridge is a version of Leo Fender's vintage six-pivot-screw vibrato type and requires a .050in Allen for adjusting the height and a Pozidrive No '1' for intonation setting. The bridge has the associated knife-edge and kitchen scale springs.

■ The 40.80mm nut is cut from a hard black plastic.

■ The machine heads are enclosed individual 'Grover-alikes'.

■ The vibrato arm has a 0.8 thread 120 UNC.

What to look for in a 'Superstrat'

This take on the modified 'S' type is a sign of Japan's confidence in the 1990s. The Pacifica reaches beyond the cheap 'copy' to a reverent stab at improvement and individuality, especially in the pickup department. The prototypes were developed in the Yamaha Guitar Development custom shop in, California, during the early part of the '90s and featured Warmouth necks with a compound radius fingerboard (flatter at the dusty end of the fingerboard). This offers the advantage of ergonomic barre chords in the 1 to 5 positions and choke-free string bending in the 7 to 20 positions – very useful.

Specific routine maintenance

Check the neck relief (see page 41). If the truss rod needs adjustment you'll need a No '1' Phillips and tweezers to remove the unusual truss rod plug and a 5mm truss rod wrench for the rod itself. See page 42 for further guidance.

This guitar is equipped with .009–.042 strings, which is pretty standard rock'n'roll these days. When changing strings it's also worth checking the machine heads, which tend to work loose. On the Pacifica this requires a 10mm Allen wrench for the front locking nuts. Do not over-tighten them – just enough to stop the machine head moving in normal use. On this guitar all the fittings were loose!

The tuner tension screws can be loosened for string changes and tightened for stability – you'll need a No '1' Phillips.

The frets could use a simple polish, which is normal on many guitars. Take the opportunity to try some very fine abrasive paper. To do this mask the fretboard with some Stewmac fret guards. This guitar needs a 2.4mm mask.

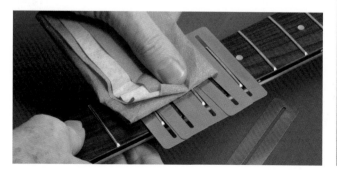

The rosewood fingerboard tends to dry out and will benefit from a little lemon oil.

If the nut snags the strings a gentle abrade with Mitchells gauged abrasive cords and a little pencil graphite should sort it. See page 44 for more on nut work.

The strap buttons may work loose with time so give them a tighten with a No '2' Phillips and if necessary plug a loose hole with a cocktail stick and some superglue – this may save your guitar from an expensive repair.

Setting string heights and intonation

The bridge is based on the classic Leo Fender design. For tips on setting up this vintage bridge see 'S' type bridge adjustment on page 58. The bridge is currently set hard to the body rather than 'floating' as originally designed, but this is easily remedied.

Under the hood

■ A minimal rout accommodates the two single coils Strat-style on the fingerboard, with the humbucker mounted to the body 'LP' style.

■ The three pickups are all high strength Alnico 5s for maximum drive, the humbucker designated JY10 M3F. One coil of the humbucker has adjustable poles for string balance adjustments, which requires a 5mm straight-slot driver.

■ Whilst you have the tools out it's worth tightening the output jack retainer. This tends to work loose, causing crackles and intermittent output. Tightening entails removing the retainer panel with a No '1' Phillips and then gripping the jack with some pliers and tightening the nut with an 11mm socket spanner.

■ The overall pickup height setting is held effectively in place by a couple of springs and needs a No '1' Pozidrive for adjustment – best done with the strings ON. See page 86 for setting optimum pickup heights. You should experiment to find the 'sweet spot' – too high and the magnets pull the strings, and too low and the pickup sounds unfocused.

■ If loose the two volume and tone knobs require a 1.9mm Allen for tightening. The pots themselves require an 11mm socket spanner (wrench) for replacement and cleaning.

■ Removing the unusual (for an 'S' type) rear panel with a No '1' Phillips reveals a small unscreened maintenance access cavity.

■ The pots are 500k type and the tone control is also a push/pull switch that shorts the 'neck side' coil of the humbucker to ground. A tiny capacitor on the tone pot also bleeds high frequencies to ground for mellow moments. The five-pole switch is a bit flimsy but does the job. A tuning fork held over the pickups is the easy way to understand the switching arrangement, which here is the usual 'five-way' arrangement (bridge/bridge and middle/middle/middle and neck / neck), except that the bridge pickup can be a humbucker or single coil depending on the position of the push/pull tone control – in this case 'up' for single coil.

Signed off

An interesting guitar that requires a little setting up and fret polishing but could easily be used professionally with a few simple modifications.

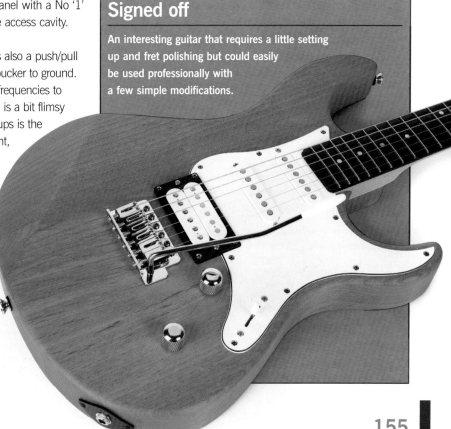

Another classic retro guitar: Eastwood Airline 2P Deluxe

This is the guitar associated with The White Stripes – though this is a modern re-issue and will probably be more practical for today's stage. It's a little pricey, but has a certain retro charm.

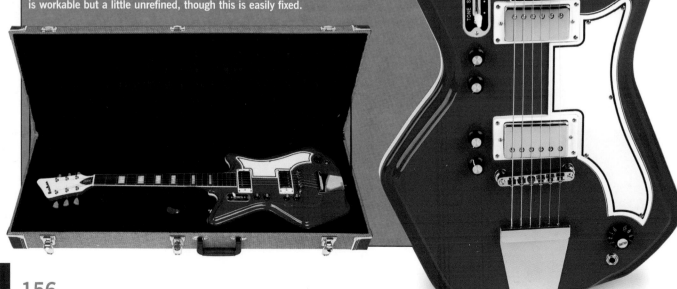

Made in Korea
Serial No.
1000150

Getting up and running

For initial learning the guitar is OK as supplied. For more enjoyment and a professional 'feel' a little attention will need to be given to the action, the frets and fretboard. Most obvious is the nut, which is set too high (see page 44), and the intonation, which is partly affected by the nut situation but also needs a little time spent on it, with a new set of strings and some attention to the Tune-O-Matic type bridge (see page 64). The neck relief is also slightly too generous (see page 41).

The first thing I suggest you do is change the factory strings for some decent .009–.042 D'Addarios, which will tune better and their light gauge will save you some strain on your digits! Spend a little time getting the guitar in tune. See page 30 for more help with this.

Condition on arrival

The guitar arrived in a nice retro 'tweed' solid case. The set-up is workable but a little unrefined, though this is easily fixed.

General description

■ The chambered mahogany body of this unusual instrument feels very light and adds a unique quality to the guitar's acoustic tone.

■ The pickguard is three-ply plastic with only five Phillips No '1' screws.

■ In true retro style there are no comfortable body contours to the eccentric body shape. Looking cool has a price! However, the body is usefully light, overall guitar weight about 7¼ lb compared with a typical 8¼lb for a Strat Vintage reissue. The body is also slightly thicker than a Strat, 1.8in compared with 1.75in. The guitar is made of mahogany sections with a heavy coat of red polyurethane.

■ The maple neck is 'bolted on' with four No '2' Phillips wood screws. It has a very usable slim oval profile and the headstock has a funky early '60s vibe with a shielded truss rod access. The original Airlines didn't have a truss rod, but instead had three screws under the neck joint so that the angle of the neck could be altered; the intention was to enable the neck pitch to be changed, but this didn't work well and most of the old vintage models have bad humps in the neck near the neck joint (as you'd expect after 50 years).

■ The machine heads are vintage Kluson copies, three-a-side type with 'jade' tulips.

■ The fingerboard is a slab of Indian rosewood with block faux 'mother of pearl' markers.

■ The bound fingerboard has an unusual string-bender friendly flat radius of 15in with a Fender-style scale length of 25½in (648mm) with 1 11/16in (42.85mm) width at the nut, which is fairly wide – good for clean arpeggios.

■ The nut is soft white plastic set a little high and with some intonation-confusing 'burrs' – easily fixed if you have the tools.

■ The bridge is a version of the classic Epiphone Tune-O-Matic and requires a 5mm straight-slot screwdriver to adjust the height and a 4mm for intonation setting.

What to look for in a working retro guitar

Looking cool is great, but any working axe also has to deliver. Go for modern pickups with some power and definition. Consider replacing any vintage hardware with modern reliable components – but keep the old bits and replace tastefully in line with the vibe!

Specific routine maintenance

Check the neck relief (see page 41). If the truss rod needs adjustment you'll require a No '1' Phillips to remove the truss rod shield and a 4mm Allen wrench for the rod itself. See page 42 for more guidance.

This guitar was supplied with .009–.046 strings, which work OK. When you're next changing strings it's worth checking the machine heads, which tend to work loose. On the Airline this requires a No '1' Phillips. Do not over-tighten them – just enough to stop the machine head moving in normal use.

The frets seem a little unfinished, which is normal on many imported guitars. Take the opportunity to polish the frets with some very fine abrasive paper. To do this, mask the fretboard with a Stewmac fret guard. This guitar needs a 2.7 mm mask.

The rosewood-type fingerboard also tends to dry out and will benefit from a little lemon oil.

The slightly unfinished nut needs a little slot work with some gauged nut files and a little finishing off to get rid of the soft plastic burrs that are bad for tone and intonation. The Mitchells abrasive cords are also gauged and help round the bottom of the slot for less snagging. See page 44 for more on nut work.

The correct neck pitch angle away from the body has been achieved at the factory with the aid of a small shim in the rear of the neck pocket (see page 62 for more on this). Note the unusual overhanging fingerboard.

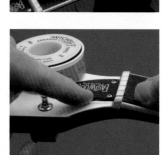

Check the neck is tightly fitted – you'll need a No '2' Phillips.

The strap buttons work loose with use, so give them a tighten with a No '1' Phillips and if necessary plug a loose hole with a cocktail stick and some superglue – this may save your guitar from a nasty plunge to earth! Check the tailpiece screws at the same time, as a loose tailpiece will cause tuning problems.

Whilst you have the tools out it's worth tightening the output jack retainer. This tends to work loose, causing crackles and intermittent output. Tightening entails using a 'Jack The Gripper' tool to hold the jack still and a 12mm socket spanner to turn the nut (see Useful contacts appendix).

Setting string heights and intonation

The bridge is based on the classic Epiphone Tune-O-Matic sitting directly on the body, supported by two height-adjustable stanchions set into a wooden block.

The original guitars had a floating wooden bridge; the hollow, fibreglass body left nowhere to mount a fixed bridge. To set up this 'modern' bridge see Tune-O-Matic type bridge adjustment on page 64.

Under the hood
Removing the pickguard using a No '1' Phillips screwdriver reveals a maintenance access cavity and the extent of the chambering. A 6in ruler disappears easily!

■ The pickups also sit over the hollow cavity and the wiring is very neatly arranged and clipped.

■ The pickups are Alnico HOT-10 humbuckers, more modern than retro. The original '60s pickups were single coil, and Airline make an optional vintage-voiced single-coil pickup available on request.

■ The pickup height setting is held in place effectively, if a little crudely, by a couple of springs and needs a No '1' Phillips for adjustment – best done with the strings ON. See page 86 for setting optimum pickup heights.

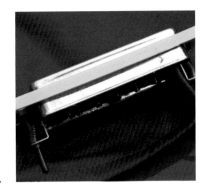

■ If loose the four individual pickup volume and tone knobs and the master volume are all push-fit, and are removable with a duster. The pots themselves require an 11mm socket spanner (wrench) for removal or adjustment.

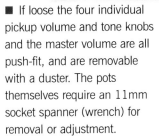

■ The tone pots are 500k-type, and these and the three-way tone switch have a small capacitor which bleeds high frequencies to ground via the two tone pots. The three-pole switch is of a PCB type more common on budget guitars. This would not be ideal for extensive professional use but is easily replaced.

Signed off

An interesting and distinctive guitar with some of the character of a Gibson but also a lighter jangly potential. Also available in left-handed, three-pickup and Bigsby-equipped versions in lots of cool colours.

Italia 'Retro 25' reverb amp

Visually at least a great retro compliment to the Airline or Danelectro guitars, this 25W transistor amp has a vintage-like spring reverb and two channels – overdrive and clean. This works OK for a classic 'garage band rehearsal'.

General description

There are many small IC-based transistor amps of this type out there, mostly in fairly bland boxes so this one is more fun. These small amps solve the 'getting started' issue for beginners but most of them struggle to really deliver a convincing sound unless you're already a good player. That said, this is good value for money and looks very cool.

Specification

■ **Inputs**
One, with two channels selected using a push button.

■ **Auxiliary input**
None.

■ **Headphone jack**
The quarter-inch headphone jack is a handy device for anyone wanting to stay on good terms with their neighbours.

■ **Channels**
Two selectable channels (normal and drive), which offer a straight 'clean' sound and an overdriven sound, with control over the amount of overdrive via the gain pot.

■ **Power handling**
25W into 8 ohms – plenty enough for most rehearsals and a small gig.

■ **Controls**
Normal volume, gain, drive select switch (LED status for each), drive volume, treble, mid, bass – the three-band EQ works very well – there is also a reverb pot.

LEFT All you need now is your Blue Suede Shoes!

Hardware

- **Cabinet material**
Open-back cabinet.

- **Handle**
Moulded cream
plastic handle.

- **Front panel**
Retro vinyl and
speaker cloth.

- **Amplifier dimensions**
Depth 22cm max (angled
front); width 42cm; height
33cm; weight 8.2kg.

- **Effects**
Reverb.

- **Speaker**
One 8in speaker.

- **Knobs**
Chicken-head knobs.
Hard-wired mains (OK
until it breaks!).

- **Outputs**
Line out – unbalanced
and on top panel; FX
send and return mono
jacks inside the cabinet's
channel-select footswitch
jack. This is not very
accessible and is unlabelled,
so it could be more user-
friendly than it is.

RIGHT Is
it a radio?

VOLUME   TREBLE   MIDDLE

Retro 25 Reverb   *Italia*

REVERB   H'PHONES

Reverb pan

As with most spring reverb equipped amps, the reverb pan is a
small rectangular metal box screwed to the bottom of the speaker
enclosure. The basic spring reverb pan is simple, with an input (think
'speaker') and output (think 'microphone') transducer, and one or
more (usually three or four) springs lightly stretched between them.
An audio feed goes in one end and comes out the other with added
'boing'. Crude but fun. As supplied, the reverb introduced acoustic
feedback even at its lowest setting. However, this turned out to be
simply a wire touching the reverb springs themselves. This 'economy'
reverb is part of an electrically unbalanced circuit and does produce a
fair amount of noise, rattle and hum. Very period correct!

Sound

The amp's clean sound is OK if a little ordinary, and the overdrive
sound is good for an IC design, though with the expected slightly
synthetic quality when compared to a true valve response.
Electric guitars need the valve frequency response, distortion and
compression that they were designed to work with (it's worth
remembering that Leo Fender designed his amplifiers first and
then designed his guitar electrics to work well with them).

Adding a simple FX unit (the retro FX from Danelectro would
preserve the period feel) can provide delay and compression etc
to really get your show on the road and get you in the right 'sound
world'. See page 112 for more sound-processing ideas.

Upgrades

I would really advise moving up to a small, inexpensive valve
amp ASAP for authentic live guitar sounds – see page 176. If
you need a retro look try the 17W Watkins Dominator or the
5W Fender Champ.

⚠ Hazard Warning

Do not venture inside guitar amplifiers unless you're qualified
to do so, and even then be sure that the mains electricity
is disconnected for some time – HT can remain stored in
capacitors and other components long after the mains is
disconnected. The amp itself is all built around one main PCB.

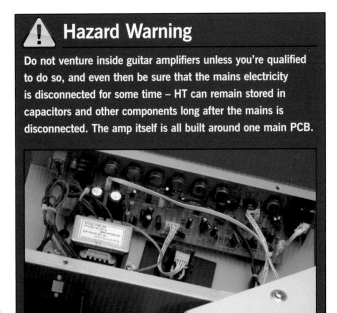

Lefties' delight: 'LP' type left-handed Encore E99 Blaster

Made in China

Serial No. 018383

So far in this book I've concentrated on right-handed guitars, but the lefties get a look in at last! This excellent starter guitar has much to offer. Based on the second most popular electric guitar in the world, it's a great classic design in an affordable starter pack that only needs a set-up.

Getting up and running

Available for £140 at the time of writing, this 'starter pack' guitar arrives with a very small and 10W transistor amp worth about £20, so that solves a common beginners' problem – electric guitars don't really function on their own (see page 164 for more). The kit also includes a plectrum, gig bag, tuner, guitar lead, guitar strap, one Allen key (for the truss rod), some strings, a guitar stand and a 'Play Now' DVD – very impressive, and potentially saving you about £30.

Don't leave the shop or website without buying a decent set of strings – even if the fitted ones have survived the trip from China they'll be cheap and will have settled into the shape of the nut and saddles – which both currently need a little work. The classic shape is classically heavy at 9.2lb. The body is mostly basswood with a wutong cap. The humbuckers are ceramic magnet 'Guitar Techs' by Trevor Wilkinson.

Tech Tip

'You can get great tone out of ceramics if you balance the coil resistance to the extra gauss from the ceramic magnets, and that's what we do; so we can supply a good sounding pickup at a budget price.'

Trevor Wilkinson

General description

■ The headstock has a break angle of 15° – not as generous and tone-enhancing as a Gibson. The plastic nut is 42mm wide.

■ Unusually for an 'LP' the guitar has a bolt-on neck, but Gibson do this themselves on their 'student' Les Paul. The bolts or wood screws require a No '2' Phillips screwdriver.

■ The maple neck has a bulky '50s-like C profile and features a fairly flat 10in radius fingerboard and a Gibson-like 24¾in scale length.

■ The truss rod is accessed under a plastic shield and requires an Allen key.

■ The floating scratchplate is secured traditionally with two No '1' Phillips screws and one No '1' bolt.

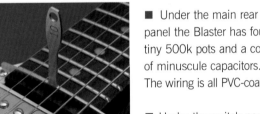

■ The guitar electrics have the usual 'LP' two-volume two-tone layout. The pots are secured with a 10mm Allen wrench.

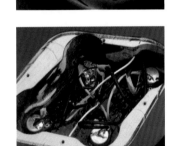

■ Under the main rear panel the Blaster has four tiny 500k pots and a couple of minuscule capacitors. The wiring is all PVC-coated.

■ Under the switch panel there is an economy switch that can easily be replaced by a pro version if necessary.

■ The bridge is an Epiphone-like Tune-O-Matic with stoptail.

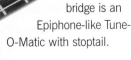

Signed off

The guitar sounds fine – even if I can only manage three chords 'upside down'. It's also available in Sunburst (but only in the right-hand version at present). Excellent value for money.

Encore Blaster 10W amp

A tiny two-channel – overdrive and clean – 'desktop' amp,
supplied as part of the Encore Blaster pack with the Blaster
'LP' guitar just described.

General description

There are many small IC-based transistor
amps, but few this compact. It solves the
'getting started' issue for beginners, being
ideal for a home practice, good value for
money and very portable.

ABOVE Simple,
but effective.

Specification

■ **Inputs**
One, with two channels selected
using a push button.

■ **Auxiliary input**
None.

■ **Headphone jack**
The quarter-inch headphone jack
is a handy device for anyone wanting
to practice in the office.

■ **Channels**
Two Selectable Channels (normal and
drive), which offer a straight 'clean'
sound and an overdriven sound, with
control over the amount of overdrive
via the gain pot.

■ **Power handling**
10W into 8 ohms – plenty for a practice
amp, but not enough projection for
a rehearsal with a band.

■ **Controls**
Normal volume,
gain, drive select
switch, volume,
treble and bass.

Hardware

■ **Cabinet material**
Open-back cabinet.

■ **Handle**
Plastic handle.

■ **Front panel**
Strong speaker grille.

■ **Amplifier dimensions**
Depth 12cm max; width 24cm; height 22cm; weight 4kg.

■ **Effects**
Overdrive.

■ **Speaker**
One 10cm speaker.

■ **Knobs**
Round plastic. Hard-wired mains (OK until it breaks!).

■ **Outputs**
Headphones.

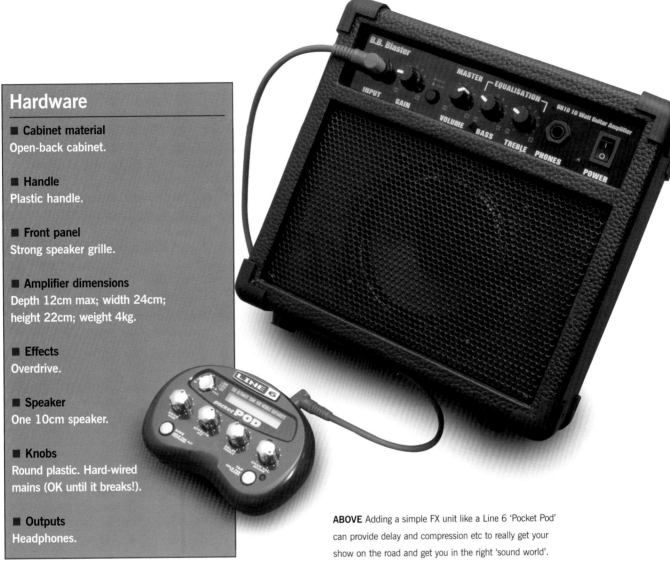

ABOVE Adding a simple FX unit like a Line 6 'Pocket Pod' can provide delay and compression etc to really get your show on the road and get you in the right 'sound world'.

Sound

The amplifier's 'clean' sound is OK, if naturally 'small'. The overdrive sound is OK for an IC design, but with the expected slightly synthetic quality when compared to a true valve response. Electric guitars need the valve frequency response, distortion and compression that they were designed to work with (Leo Fender designed his amplifiers first and then designed his guitar electrics to work well with them).

Adding a simple FX unit like a Line 6 'Pocket Pod' can provide delay and compression etc to really get your show on the road and get you in the right 'sound world'. See page 112 for more sound-processing ideas.

Upgrades

This is perfect for its purpose if that doesn't extend beyond your home office or spare bedroom. Otherwise I'd really advise moving up to a small, inexpensive 'valve' amp ASAP for authentic live guitar sounds before your first band rehearsal. See page 176.

⚠ Hazard Warning

Do not venture inside guitar amplifiers unless you're qualified to do so, and even then be sure that the mains electricity is disconnected for some time – HT can remain stored in capacitors and other components long after the mains is disconnected. The amp itself is all built around one main PCB.

Encore E375 small 'S' type

Made in China

Serial No.
023616

So far in this book I've concentrated on full-size guitars, but many younger beginners need a shorter scale length. Based on the most popular electric guitar in the world, the Blaster is a classic design that needs a considerable set-up.

Getting up and running

As supplied this guitar didn't really work. The worrying thing is that a youngster wouldn't know that, and nor would most parents. The biggest problem with smaller-size guitars is that all the usual full-size guitar intonation issues are made more critical by dint of the shorter scale length.

I spent two hours adjusting the nut, saddles and vibrato unit to achieve a workable, playable guitar, and suspect that most purchasers wouldn't want to or expect to spend that kind of time or money on a 'beginner's' instrument. The upshot is that a frustrated youngster might give up, which is bad for them and bad for the whole music industry. I know that Trev Wilkinson is working on improving the manufacturing tolerances of these guitars even as I write.

The problem is that in practice, the shorter scale length naturally produces a lower tension – which causes intonation discrepancies as the fretted notes tend to easily 'bend' sharp in normal fretting. I've never in my 45 years' experience found a three-quarter steel string guitar that plays in tune and this often puts off young pupils, as they never sound good. The problem is exacerbated by the lack of suitable three-quarter-scale strings – an issue I've taken up with the string manufacturers.

General description

■ The classic shape is very light at 4.75lb, about half the normal expected weight – which is a great plus for beginners. The body is contoured from an unnamed wood and coated in a thick layer of black polyurethane.

■ The pickups are excellent single-coil 'Guitar Tech's' by Trevor Wilkinson.

■ The headstock has a string break angle of 15° at the bass but only 8° at the first string, even with the string tree – not as generous and tone-enhancing as would be ideal. The plastic nut is a generous 42mm wide.

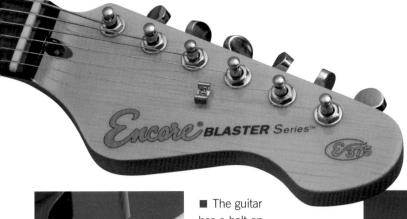

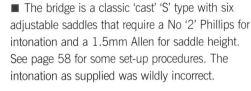

■ The bridge is a classic 'cast' 'S' type with six adjustable saddles that require a No '2' Phillips for intonation and a 1.5mm Allen for saddle height. See page 58 for some set-up procedures. The intonation as supplied was wildly incorrect.

■ The guitar has a bolt-on maple neck; the bolts or wood screws require a No '2' Phillips. The vibrato unit has the modern three-spring arrangement.

■ The vibrato springs require a No '2' Phillips for tension adjustment and a No '1' for the fulcrum screws. The vibrato arm thread is a 25G.

■ A shim was needed in the neck pocket to achieve a decent pitch.

■ The maple neck itself has a shallow 'C' profile and features a fairly flat 10in-radius rosewood fingerboard and the tiny 19in scale length. As supplied the saddles didn't reflect the fingerboard radius – part of the intonation problem.

■ The truss rod is accessed at the headstock and requires a 4mm Allen wrench.

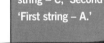

■ The scratchplate is a nice pearly take on the classic shape, secured traditionally with eight No '1' Phillips screws.

■ The guitar electrics have the usual 'S'-type 'one volume, two tone' layout. The pots are secured with a 10mm Allen wrench.

■ Under the hood is a large 'swimming pool' arrangement that almost goes through to the vibrato spring cavity.

■ The Blaster has three tiny 250k pots and one minuscule 223J capacitor. The wiring is all PVC coated. There's an economy PU selector switch that can easily be replaced by a pro version if necessary.

Signed off

There's a gap in the market for well-intonated three-quarter electric strings, as several major manufacturers make three-quarter-scale electrics, including Fender. The supplied strings are .011–.052, which helps give a little more tension to the short scale.

The guitar's sounds are good, but the intonation, string type and factory set-up issues need addressing if many young guitarists are to be dissuaded from simply giving up. Trevor Wilkinson himself has plans to retool this guitar ASAP to achieve better intonation results, particularly in the first position.

At present JHS make the following suggestion: 'For ease of playing and in order to ensure that the guitar intonates correctly, we recommend that you tune the E375 guitar to "A" tuning, rather than standard "E" tuning: 'Sixth string – A, 'Fifth string – D, 'Fourth string – G, 'Third string – C, 'Second string – E, 'First string – A.'

Turn it up to eleven! Vintage: 'The Reaper' Flying V metal axe

I've taught a few surreal guitar classes in my time, with ten-year-old boys learning their first three chords on 'Flying V' lookalikes. Primary school classrooms never have enough monitors to stick your boot on!

Made in the Far East

Serial No
109022787

Getting up and running
Plug and play! For more enjoyment and a professional 'feel' a little attention could be given to the frets and fretboard. A new set of strings and a fret polish should do the job. But first spend a little time getting the guitar in tune – see page 30 for help with this.

Condition on arrival

The beast arrived caged in a simple cardboard box. The factory set-up is workable and ready to rock.

General description

■ The truncated 'V' is eye-catching and the eastern poplar body also benefits from some interesting 'aged' inlays. The Reaper has no pickguard, so windmill with care. In true retro style there are no comfortable body contours to the eccentric body shape but you can play this one sitting down – although that might be missing the point!

■ The guitar is quite light, at about 8lb compared with a typical 8¼lb for a Strat Vintage reissue. The body is about the same thickness as a Strat at 1.7in.

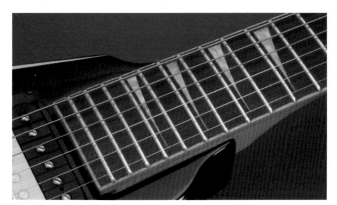

■ The fingerboard is a slab of Indian rosewood with pearloid Sail-Fin markers. It has the heavy metal 'string-bender friendly' flat radius of 15in, with a Gibson-style scale length of 24¾in/628mm and a wide 43mm nut – good for clean arpeggios. The headstock pitch is 12°, enough to keep the strings in place.

■ The 24-fret maple neck gives you two full octaves and is 'bolted on' with four No '2' Phillips wood screws Fender-style. The neck has a very fast slim oval profile and the headstock has a funky Gibson Explorer vibe with a shielded truss rod access.

■ The bridge is a version of the classic Epiphone-type Tune-O-Matic and stop bar, made in Korea by Sungill (a BM002) and requires a 5mm straight-slot for adjusting the height and intonation setting. The stop bar needs to be set low enough to give a good break angle but not too low to cause string breakages (there's usually a happy medium) – you'll need a 10mm straight-slot screwdriver. The bridge also has the retaining spring associated with the later Gibson ABR1. It's important this isn't lost, a common cause of rattles and buzz.

■ The nut is cut from hard black plastic. See below and page 44 for more on nut work.

■ The machine heads are all-black Wilkinson WJ05s, six in a row.

What to look for in a 'shape' guitar

Looking dangerous isn't enough! You need some overwound humbuckers and preferably a 'dive-bomb' capable trem and locking nut. These could be retrofitted to an initial economy guitar, given a solid enough basic construction. The Flying V is the ultimate 'shape' guitar, but for most aspirant Warlocks the original '50s Gibsons are out of reach financially, and when seen close up may even look a little dated. This affordable axe has updated the vibe and is Trev Wilkinson-powered for all the Kerrang! you can handle.

Specific routine maintenance

Check the neck relief (see page 41). If the truss rod requires adjustment you'll need a No '0' Phillips screwdriver to remove the truss rod shield and a 4mm Allen wrench for the rod itself. See page 42 for further guidance.

This guitar was supplied with .010–.046 strings, which work well. When you're next changing strings it's worth checking the machine heads, which tend to work loose. On the Reaper this requires a No '1' Phillips for the back screws and a 10mm Allen wrench for the front locking nuts. Don't over-tighten them – just enough to stop the machine head moving in normal use.

The tuner tension screws can be loosened for string changes and tightened for stability – you'll need a No '1' Phillips.

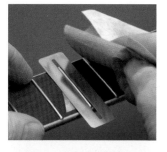

The correct neck pitch angle away from the body has been achieved with an accurate neck pocket at the factory. There are no shims required.

The frets just need a simple polish, which is normal on many guitars. Take the opportunity to try some very fine abrasive paper. To do this, mask the fretboard with a Stewmac fret guard. This guitar needs a 2.7mm mask. The rosewood-type fingerboard also tends to dry out and will benefit from a little lemon oil.

The nut snags the strings a little, but a gentle abrade with Mitchells abrasive cords and a dab of Planet Waves' Lubrikit should sort that. See page 44 for more on nut work.

See page 44 for more on nut work.

Setting string heights and intonation

The bridge is based on the classic Epiphone Tune-O-Matic sitting directly on the body supported, by two height-adjustable stanchions set into the solid body. For tips on setting up this 'modern' bridge see Tune-O-Matic type bridge adjustment on page ??.

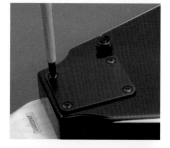

Always check that the neck is tightly fitted – you'll need a No '2' Phillips. A loose neck naturally plays havoc with tone and intonation.

The unusually placed strap buttons may work loose with use so give them a tighten with a No '2' Phillips and if necessary plug a loose hole with a cocktail stick and some superglue. This may save your guitar from a nasty plunge to earth!

Whilst you have the tools out it's worth tightening the output jack retainer. This tends to work loose, causing crackles and intermittent output. Tightening entails removing the jack panel with a No '0' Phillips and then gripping the jack with some pliers and tightening the nut with a 12mm socket spanner.

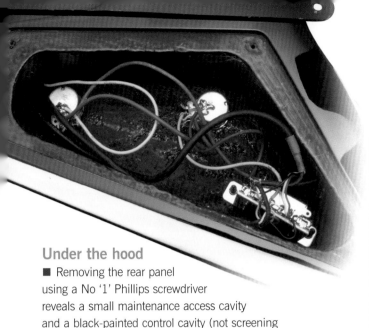

Under the hood

■ Removing the rear panel using a No '1' Phillips screwdriver reveals a small maintenance access cavity and a black-painted control cavity (not screening paint, which might help reduce induced noise).

■ The pots are 500k type and the tone control has an anonymous capacitor which bleeds the high frequencies to ground. The five-pole switch is of a PCB type more common on budget guitars. This would not be ideal for extensive use but is easily replaced.

■ The overall pickup height setting is held effectively in place by a couple of springs and needs a No '1' Phillips for adjustment – best done with the strings ON. See page 86 for setting optimum pickup heights. You should experiment to find the 'sweet spot' – too high and the magnets pull the strings, too low and the pickup sounds unfocused.

■ If loose the two black volume and tone knobs are push-fit – safely removable with a duster wrapped under the rim. The pots themselves require an 11mm socket spanner (wrench) for replacement and cleaning. Disappointingly they only go up to ten.

■ The pickups, accessed with a No '1' Phillips, are Wilkinson WVHZ B&N (bridge and neck) humbuckers, made to a similar spec to Gibson PAFs, with plenty of middle-frequency grunt. The black coil of the 'Zebra' bobbins has adjustable poles for string balance adjustments, which requires a 4mm straight-slot screwdriver. The pickups are four-wire types with plenty of scope for series/parallel, 'Split coil' and out-of-phase switching. They're currently wired for either humbucker or single coil operation via the five-way switch, which is very useful – two classic sounds from one guitar.

Signed off

An interesting and distinctive guitar with some of the character of the classic Gibson, but also a clear identity of its own. The guitar is also available in plain black with a Floyd Rose trem.

Be aware that the black paint applied to all the screws and fittings comes off at the slightest touch of any tools, which may lead to a little tatty appearance!

You'll certainly need a large Marshall amp, some dry ice and a monitor for your left boot to fully reap the benefit of this instrument. Kerrrrang!

Second-hand bargain: Classic Epiphone 'SG' G400

Introduced in 1960, the Gibson version of this guitar has carved itself a significant niche in rock history. With its AC/DC and 'School of Rock' associations, it is popular with teenage rockers.

Getting up and running

For more enjoyment and a professional 'feel' a little attention could be given to the frets and fretboard. A new set of strings, a fret polish and a little bridge adjustment should do the job. If you need help with tuning and intonation, see pages 64 and 30.

Condition on arrival

Though second-hand this guitar is in 'nearly new' condition and presents a bargain. Second-hand doesn't always mean second best, and every first-time buyer should consider the 'previously loved' option – there are bargains to be had; but try and get expert guidance, and don't buy blind on the Internet! This guitar is from the stock of trusted specialist retailer Macari's, an institution on London's Charing Cross Road habituated over time by the likes of Jimi Hendrix, Eric Clapton, John Entwistle and Jimmy Page – they never shied away from second-hand bargains, so neither should we!

Since October 2002 all non-USA Epiphones have been made at Qingdao Gibson, a factory near Qingdao in China. This plant is dedicated to only making Epiphone guitars. Gibson were the first US guitar company with their own factory in Asia. Overall average standards are currently exceptionally high.

The instrument arrived in a simple cardboard box. The set-up is perfectly workable and ready to rock. There's a small crack in one of the pickup surrounds, but this is easily replaced with improved parts availability via the Internet.

General Description

■ The guitar has the classic Gibson SG shape and appointments from 1962, and is finished in something very close to the classic Cherry colour. The guitar is light, at about 7½lb compared with a typical 8¼lb for a Strat Vintage reissue. The three-piece body is typically thinner than a Strat at 1.4in, but with very little contour.

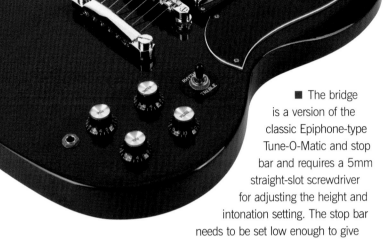

■ The two-piece 22-fret neck gives you almost two full octaves and is set and glued in traditional SG style. The neck has a fairly slim oval profile – I've seen much slimmer on SGs – but it works OK. The headstock has an interesting inlay and a Gibson truss rod shield!

■ The nut is cut from a hard black plastic.

■ The machine heads are individual modern Grovers – heavier than the traditional Klusons but potentially more stable.

■ The fingerboard is a slab of wide-grained Indian rosewood with traditional trapezoid markers and a flat bend-friendly radius of 15in (381mm), with a Gibson-style scale length of 24¾in (628mm) and a 41.8mm nut. The tone-enhancing headstock pitch is 14° – wood-savingly achieved by gluing on a separate headstock.

■ The bridge is a version of the classic Epiphone-type Tune-O-Matic and stop bar and requires a 5mm straight-slot screwdriver for adjusting the height and intonation setting. The stop bar needs to be set low enough to give a good break angle but not too low to cause string breakages (there's usually a happy medium) – you'll need a 10mm straight-slot. The bridge also has the retaining spring associated with the later Gibson ABR1. It's important that this isn't lost – a cause of rattles and buzz.

■ Be aware that the Tune-O-Matic and stop bar are traditionally held in place by string tension alone – a couple of elastic bands prevent any damage to the finish whilst maintaining the guitar.

What to look for in an SG

This classic design is spotlighted at the front of this manual, but you need to be especially aware that the previously unprecedented fingerboard access of the SG design makes for a potentially unstable unsupported neck. So you need to check this before you buy: does the pitch of the strings change as you handle the neck? Good SGs have a very solid (often mahogany) neck.

Specific routine maintenance

Check the neck relief (see page 41). If the truss rod requires adjustment you'll need a No '1' Phillips to remove the truss rod shield and a 9/32in truss rod wrench for the rod itself. See page 42 for more guidance.

This guitar is equipped with .009–.042 strings which work fine, though many people prefer .010s on this scale length

When you're changing strings it's also worth checking the machine heads, which tend to work loose. On the SG this requires a No '1' Phillips for the back screws and a 10mm Allen wrench for the front locking nuts. Do not over-tighten them – just enough to stop the machine head moving in normal use. All the fittings were loose!

The tuner tension screws can be loosened for string changes and tightened for stability. You'll need a No '1' Phillips.

Being second-hand, the frets show a little wear but not enough to cause problems yet, and just need a polish, which is normal on many guitars. Take the opportunity

to try some very fine abrasive paper. To do this, mask the fretboard with a Stewmac fret guard. This guitar needs a 2.7mm mask.

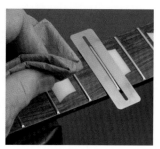

The rosewood fingerboard also needs a clean – a lot of dead flesh accumulates on fingerboards! Some Dunlop 01 will loosen this up. The board also tends to dry out and will benefit from a little lemon oil.

If the nut snags the strings, a gentle abrade with Mitchells gauged abrasive cords and a dab of Planet Waves' Lubrikit should sort that. See page 44 for more on nut work.

The strap buttons may work loose with use so give them a tighten with a No '1' Phillips and if necessary plug a loose hole with a cocktail stick and some superglue. This may save your guitar from an expensive repair.

Setting string heights and intonation

The bridge is based on the classic Epiphone Tune-O-Matic and stop bar, sitting directly on the body supported by two stanchions set into the solid body. For tips on setting-up this type of bridge see Tune-O-Matic type bridge adjustment on page 64.

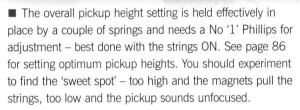

Under the hood

■ Whilst you have the tools out it's worth tightening the output jack retainer. This tends to work loose, causing crackles and intermittent output. Tightening entails removing the foil-screened rear panel with a No '1' Phillips and then gripping the jack with some pliers and tightening the nut with a half-inch socket spanner.

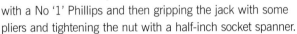

■ Removing the rear panel reveals a small maintenance access cavity and a screening painted surface which will help reduce induced noise. The electrical continuity on the screening paint is consistently good.

■ The pots are 500k type and the two tone controls have small 2A 223J capacitors that bleed the high frequencies to ground. The three-pole switch is a bit flimsy and produces electrical crackles – this would not be ideal for professional use but is easily cleaned or replaced.

■ The two Alnico V pickups are Epiphone humbuckers, designated 'HOTCH (G)1 LP BRIDGE' and '57 CH G Dot LP neck'. One coil of the twin bobbins has adjustable poles for string balance adjustments, which requires a 4mm straight-slot screwdriver. The pickups are simple two-wire types. The cavities are also screen-painted but these are not as yet grounded.

■ The overall pickup height setting is held effectively in place by a couple of springs and needs a No '1' Phillips for adjustment – best done with the strings ON. See page 86 for setting optimum pickup heights. You should experiment to find the 'sweet spot' – too high and the magnets pull the strings, too low and the pickup sounds unfocused.

■ The cracked pickup surround is easily replaced with an equivalent from Axetec Guitar Pickups & Parts (info@axetec. co.uk). This is a simple 'drop in and replace' – just ensure that the springs are mounted 'taper down', and that the mounting ring sits at the 'wide end' of the wedge nearer the bridge.

■ If loose the two black volume and tone knobs are push-fit – safely removable with a duster wrapped under the rim. The pots themselves require an 11mm socket spanner (wrench) for replacement and cleaning.

Signed off

An interesting guitar with some of the character of the classic Gibson. Also available in plain ebony. The ideal practice companion has to be the Epiphone Valve Junior (see overleaf). Guitar/amp matching is an interesting area – when it's right, you get great sound without resort to effects boxes.

Epiphone 'Valve Junior' 5W amp

A terrific recent development is the arrival of small, affordable valve guitar amps from Fender, Marshall and a host of other manufacturers. I've personally found this Epiphone extremely useful as a practice amp and even used it on a few gigs (via the PA).

'Radio Shack' roots

Electric guitars were conceived in the valve era of the 1930s to 1960s, and their gloriously primitive electro-magnetic designs work best when they're coupled to the primeval electronics of a simple class A amplifier (whether true class A or actually class AB doesn't really matter).

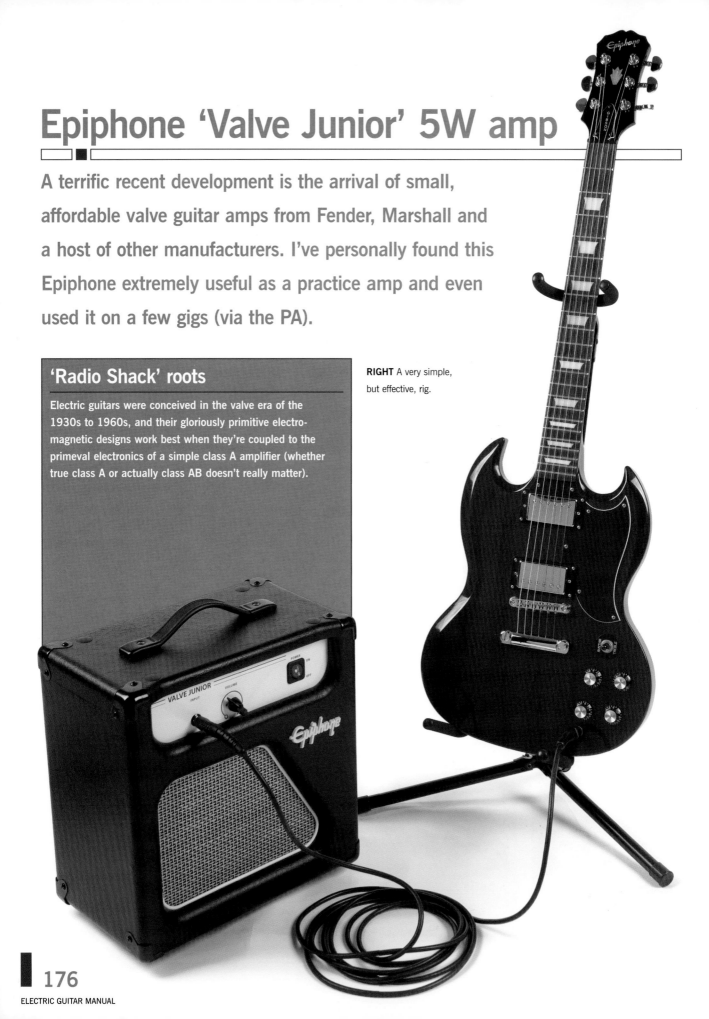

RIGHT A very simple, but effective, rig.

General description

■ This is a very small 'class A' valve amp employing two Russian-made Sovtek valves, a 12AX7 and an EL84.

LEFT One jack socket and one knob. Perfect!

■ The amp measures 14.6in x 8.7in x 15.1in (370mm x 220mm x 384mm) and the birch ply cab weighs 20.9lb total.

■ Most of the original-spec amps come now with an Eminence 8in speaker and the output is rated at 5W.

■ In any home practice situation this is more than adequate, and miked up through a PA the amp delivers a terrific gutsy sound – especially with a little reverb etc from a digital FX box.

■ The minimalist approach means the amp has one control (volume) which is fine – Leo Fender's first amp didn't even have that.

■ The low power means you get all the graunch of a cranked up valve amp without the ear damage. Eric Clapton's *Layla* was recorded on a similar amp (a Vintage Fender Champ).

■ The rear panel has a 4ohm speaker output, meaning you can use an alternative cab if you wish.

■ Many enthusiasts upgrade the speaker to an Italian-made Jensen and the valves to pro-grade Harmas, available in the UK from Watford Valves. This is a simple and effective changeover costing approximately £45.

■ Note the hefty transformer – key to the sound of a good valve amp.

There are plenty of similar amps available at present and more models appear every month. This specific example simply serves as a guide to the features required for cheap, affordable tone.

> ⚠ **Hazard Warning**
>
> Do not venture inside guitar amplifiers unless you're qualified to do so, and even then be sure that the mains electricity has been disconnected.

Key players and their instruments

In the middle of the last century the solid-body electric guitar truly arrived, and its distinctive sounds changed popular music forever. Ironically, in 1950 Leo Fender had been simply trying to make 'Western Swing' guitarists audible above the hubbub of brass and fiddles, yet with his Broadcaster he accidently designed the perfect rock'n'roll guitar.

In a parallel quest, since 1941 Les Paul and Epiphone had been trying to make instrumental guitar music heard on the radio and embryonic TV. With Gibson's help their Goldtop 'Les Paul' would surface in 1952. The world would never be the same again.

LEFT Guitar heroes! Jimmy Hendrix, Joe Satriani, Angus Young, T Bone Walker.

RIGHT A '50s-vibe Squier Tele.

The 'rock guitar' pioneers

Most 'rock guitar' is founded on earthy catchy riffs rooted in the blues. For this groundwork much credit has to go to Hubert Sumlin (b1931, Greenwood, Mississippi), recording with the Muddy Waters and Howlin' Wolf bands, for his definitive *Smokestack Lightnin'*, *Killin' Floor* and *Spoonful*. Hubert had (and still has) a 1955 P90-equipped Les Paul Goldtop and a Louis Electric Model HS M12 amplifier.

The idea of an electric blues 'solo' was defined and refined by T-Bone Walker (born 1910, Linden, Texas, died 1975), BB King (born 1925, Itta Bena, Mississippi), Otis Rush (born 1935, Philadelphia, Mississippi), Freddie King (born 1934, Dallas, Texas, died 1976), and Buddy Guy (born 1936, Lettsworth, Louisiana). These guys took the guitar further by developing the pentatonic riffs of the rural blues into extended instrumental solos and features.

BB King's *Lucille* has most often been played on a Gibson with a Fender twin amp – most of the other blues players have played the American trilogy of Strats, Teles and Seth Lover-equipped Gibsons (Les Pauls, Flying Vs and semis), often coupled with a Fender amp.

The rock'n'roll smorgasbord drew on these blues roots but added the country and steel guitar influences of Speedy West and Jimmy Bryant's Telecaster, alongside western swing and the groundbreaking intros of Louis

Chuck Berry.

B.B. King.

Jordan's guitarist, Carl Hogan. Scotty Moore (born 1931, Gadsden, Tennessee) spiced up Elvis Presley's rockabilly with a traditional Gibson 'Jazz box' and lost out to James Burton (born 1939, Dubberly, Louisiana) who fired a Tele from the hip from day one. Cliff Gallup (born 1930, died 1988), who played in Gene Vincent's Blue Caps, favoured an early Gretsch Duo Jet with De Armond pickups and a Standel 25L15 26W tube amp with a single 15-inch speaker.

The English take on all this Americana can't be overestimated. British players like Hank Marvin (born 1941) and Jeff Beck (born 1944) heard the whole American scene from the outside, grabbing whatever vinyl crumbs could be picked up on AM radio and in import record shops. So they heard James Burton, Hubert Sumlin and Les Paul on a level playing field, without America's wasteful racial segregation. Eric Clapton heard the fiery instrumentals of Freddie King alongside the acoustic lament of Robert Johnson and neither knew nor probably cared if these guys were white, black, brown or green, as long as they made that extraordinary music. In Liverpool in the 1960s my all-white band played Chuck Berry and Muddy Waters to all-black audiences, and none of us could find a rhyme for 'irony'. Down the road John Lennon's Quarrymen did the same.

Technically the tape echo devices of early rock'n'roll – often just a spare tape recorder with the record and playback heads contributing a fluttering delay – were very influential, and Hank Marvin would take his Meazzi echo and AC15 Vox to the top of the 1960 charts with a string of all-guitar hits, starting with Jerry Lordan's *Apache*.

This is a bit of a diversion, but Hank Marvin, with the Shadows, had a huge impact on the British scene pre-Beatles, and I have always been intrigued as to why he initially went that weird solo guitar instrumental route. So I asked him (this is music history first-hand from one who was there!):

'In 1959, on Cliff Richards' first album, recorded live at Abbey Road, we recorded two instrumentals – *Driftin'* and *Jet Black* – and later recorded them as a single. The success of Duane Eddy, who had a bunch of hits beginning with *Rebel Rouser* in 1958, and of Russ Conway, who was "happening" with his piano instrumentals, encouraged us to record those two tracks. We hadn't heard of The Ventures, who hadn't as yet appeared on the UK scene – they seemed to break in the USA, with *Walk Don't Run*, at about the same time as *Apache* was a hit in UK. So they weren't an influence. We considered ourselves a vocal/instrumental group like the Crickets, and the Everly Brothers. After our first tour of the USA in January and February 1960 we met the songwriter Jerry Lordan. Jerry asked us if we were recording soon and, "Would we consider an instrumental?" "Possibly!" Jerry took out his ukulele and strummed and sang an instrumental for Jet Harris and myself. It was sensational. We got Bruce Welch and Tony Meeham to listen, and they agreed with us. We arranged it and I happened to come up with the intro, which, of course, most people think is part of the tune – not so!

'With the success of *Apache* we became primarily an instrumental group with the occasional vocal single. Interestingly, in 1965 we had a big hit with a vocal, *Don't Make My Baby Blue*, and at that time, when he was chatting with me at Abbey Road, George Harrison told me how much he liked that record and advised us to go in that direction and give up the instrumentals. Was he right or was he wrong? Answers on a postcard please!'

Anyone who underestimates the Shadows' importance to the development of rock guitar need only refer to *The Beatles Anthology* and *Cry For a Shadow* (Harrison/Lennon, 1961). Every British rock guitarist came under the spell of Hank Marvin and every American fell under the spell of the Beatles, Jeff Beck, Eric Clapton, Peter Green and Jimmy Page.

Back in the early 1960s those guitarists who couldn't afford Gibsons and Fenders took to Kays, Guyatones and Danelectros – now all collectables for their distinct sound, despite poorer overall mechanics. In the UK and Europe it was 'make do and mend', with copy guitars from Hofner and Futurama.

George Harrison (1943–2001) had sought a Fender Stratocaster in 1961, but when pipped at the post by another Liverpool player settled for

Hank Marvin with The Shadows.

a Gretsch Duo Jet – American guitars were illegal imports in austere post-war Britain. George's major pentatonic riffs were eventually played on Gretsch 'Country Gentlemen' and 12-string Rickenbackers, through Vox AC30s and AC 100 valve amps. He would at last acquire a Strat, a rosewood Tele and a Les Paul for the Beatles' later studio masterpieces, along with many Fender amps.

When Jeff Beck paired his Fender Esquire with a 'Tone Bender' (fuzz box), and Eric Clapton his Freddie King-inspired Les Paul with a Marshall, the defining sound of modern rock guitar was created. As these guys re-exported blues-based rock to America, the USA slowly woke up to its own home-grown riches – 'the three Kings', Buddy Guy and a host of others were 'rediscovered'.

Mike Bloomfield came under the same spell with his Les Paul and valve Fenders. John Mayall's 'pub blues' gave the world Peter Green and Mick Taylor, both Les Paul and Marshall fans. Jimmy Page and Gary Moore took the whole thing further and louder. The era of Seth Lover's humbucker had arrived – not just 'bucking the hum' but driving valves to sweet overload.

The USA roll call includes the immortal Jimi Hendrix (1942–70), who in 1966 threw away the rulebook with a then out-of-fashion Stratocaster and a mind-expanding pair of Marshall stacks. Significantly, Jimi came to multicultural Britain to make his breakthrough, with the help of the extended sound palette of Roger Mayer's Octavia, the Arbiter Fuzz Face and a Vox Wah Wah.

All these guys and countless others set the stage for electric rock guitarists, and established the bedrock for everything that has followed.

A second wave

In the 1970s Brian May and David Gilmour – both players who had their roots in the '60s – further extended the guitar hero's role. The melodic possibilities of a sustained guitar sound aided by every kind of overdrive were explored and analogue delayed. Brian May even built his own guitar, based on Burns electronics and a mahogany fireplace, with much help from emerging custom luthiers like John Diggins. Most players, however, stayed with Fender and Gibson, but experimented with overwound pickups and upgraded components.

Heavy metal saw the rise of the long-necked SG and the 'shape guitar', the 'flying V' and pink spandex – set your phallic symbol for the heart of the glitter ball – along with stadium rock, bigger amps and the first proper PA. 'Hello Boston ... are we all having fun?'

The '80s saw rock guitarists striving for sustain without too much overdrive. Mark Knopfler resurrected the pink Strat (again) and showed just how versatile the vulgar plank could

Mark Knopfler.

Brian May.

be – less overdrive, more compression. Mark also led the rise of the 'boutique guitar', with a fabulous line in Pensa Suhrs – the Rolls Royce of guitars and the versatility of Paul Reed Smith, no expense spared. The classic instruments remained to the fore, the album went compact, and any delay in release was digital.

The '90s saw the resurgence of guitar-based bands, with the Red Hot Chilli Peppers and Green Day featuring riff-based songs. Forget the record player and dump it on your iPod.

We begin the 21st century with an established genre and the instruments to support it. The relic phenomenon tells us a lot about a craving for the classics – the battered Strat and the time-worn Tele, the 'lost' Les Paul from the golden era of 1958–60 – they're all in the custom shop, along with a road-worn Mexican.

Perhaps the greatest boon is availability. *All* the classic guitars of the '50s are currently available, and in many respects these are often better than the originals. CNC technology offers consistency and more discriminating players pressure for quality control. You can have a '62 Fiesta Red Strat if you like, battered or plain – you pays your dollars, you takes your choice.

The first wave of players had established the sound of the 'S', 'T', 'SG' and 'LP' types, with side riffs from Rickenbacker and Gretsch. A mellow Gibson 330 and 335 were always available to sweeten the mix. Now Jack White has led the rediscovery of Airline and other retro delights, Danelectro, Jazzmasters and Jaguars. You can't make a pop video without a Gretsch White Falcon!

The virtuoso cult of Joe Satriani and Steve Vai has pushed the guitars' technical development, with seven-string instruments and slack tuning and even the return of the baritone guitar. Super Strats have hotter pickups and indestructible trems. The once flat fingerboard is steeply radiused, flatter or 'compound' – your choice.

Seymour Duncan and a host of others make every kind of pickup available – a dozen shades of humbucker and a single coil that invisibly 'bucks the hum', classic FiltaTrons from TV Jones, and active pickups in 14 flavours and a free PP3.

Digital guitars and self-tuning robots, the rise and resurrection of 'Roland ready' and the undead synth! It's all out there, and as guitarists the challenge for us is to get the best from it all, to revel in the variety and strive to play one earth-stopping solo before we too march off to the great gig in the sky. Remember, you only need to know two things – all the chords and all the scales (I'm still working on it). Enjoy the ride, find your voice, put down that Allen key and wail.

Slash in action.

Jimmy Page.

GU

HOT ROCK

DISK

rocks

8 Classic rock songs.

Albatross – Fleetwood Mac

Californication – Red Hot Chili Peppers

Enter Sandman – Metallica

Highway To Hell – AC/DC

I

Res

Su

lassic rock so

out Love - Van

- Oasis

Appendices, glossary and contacts

This is a great time to learn the guitar. The hardware is cheap, and the teaching resources fantastic.

LEFT Rockschool 'Hot Rock'. It's never been easier to learn.

RIGHT An Ibanez Artcore AF75TDG-IV.

Learning resources

The rock guitar pioneers struggled to get help learning guitar – there were very few resources in the 1950s and '60s, and almost no teachers. How things have changed! You can now study for a BA degree in electric guitar. However, several of the 'case study' guitars in this book arrived with a well-meaning brochure on finding a teacher (great), and an instructional handout pointing 'Flying V' purchasers towards the merits of *She'll be Coming Round the Mountain When she Comes*, played in 'Cowboy Chords in the first position'. This seems a little absurd, especially as the bigger learning resource picture these days is literally fantastic.

The graded *Rockschool* books not only get guitarists started with a range of idioms from Brit Pop to Jazz Funk, but also offer pro backing tracks from a real band recorded on CD. (ISBN 978-1-902775-36-4 is for Grade I–VIII.)

The *Totally Interactive Guitar Bible* from Jawbone Press is an astonishing beginner's course, including a CD, a DVD, a four-colour book and about five years of study notes in TAB and notation. (ISBN 978-1-87154-778-8.)

The 'Jam With' and 'In Session With' series from Total Accuracy Professional Guitar Workshops include Hank Marvin, Buddy Holly, Santana, Satriani, the Beatles etc, each comprising TAB and CD.

A note about TAB limitations

The ancient lute tablature form often used by guitarists is useful for indicating fingerings about the guitar, but is not so good for developing general musicianship. I strongly recommend that any serious student of the guitar should also learn modern music notation for reading rhythms, and thereby share a common language with every other trained musician you'll ever meet. I've worked on literally thousands of sessions for records, TV and radio and I've never seen a TAB notation presented. Arrangers tend to be keyboard orientated and consequently use standard notation – so be prepared, and enjoy sharing all the world's written music.

Essential Elements Book 1 from Hal Leonard (ISBN 978-0634054341) is good for 'three-chord trick' versions of Elvis and Robert Johnson as well as for learning standard notation without pain!

Guys Grids and Guys Scales are a fantastic lifetime resource! (ISBN 978-0-615-31295-8 for grids.)

Berklee Press' *Instant Guitar* by Tomo Fujita is a great starting point for basic rock guitar (the new edition has a different cover from that shown). (ISBN 978-0634029516.)

Finally, many great sites have evolved on the Internet with video and TAB resources.

It's all out there – just ask!

New off the press in 2011 are the new Rockschool 'Hot Rock; books. These offer 'easy' and 'complete' versions of many classic tracks with reliable notation and TAB – see page 184.

■ **Appendix 2**
Capacitor codes

It's worth knowing how to read all the different codes found on your guitar's capacitors, with a view to experimenting with different values.

Large body capacitors usually have the value printed on the body of the cap – for example, 100μF 250V.

Start here for the smaller non-polarised and old-type capacitors.

The smaller caps have two or three numbers printed on them, some with one or two letters added to that value.

As you can see, it all looks very simple. If a capacitor is marked like this, '105', it just means 10 + 5 zeros = 10 + 00000 = 1,000,000pF = 1,000nF = 1μF. And that's exactly the way you write it, too. Value is always in pF (picofarads). The letter added to the value is the tolerance, and in some cases a second letter is the temperature coefficient, mostly only used in military applications or industrial components.

If you have a ceramic capacitor with '474J' printed on it, it means 47 + 4 zeros = 470,000 = 470,000pF, J = 5% tolerance (470,000pF = 470nF = 0.47μF). The only major thing to remember here is to move the decimal point back six places for μF and three for nf. The table below is a simple version for direct conversions to make it easier for you:

Code	Decipher	Value (pf)	Value (nf)	Value (μf)
102	10 + 00	1,000pf	1nf	0.001μf
103	10 + 000	10,000pf	10nf	0.01μf
104	10 + 0000	100,000pf	100nf	0.1μf
222	22 + 00	2,200pf	2.2nf	0.0022μf
223	22 + 000	22,000pf	22nf	0.022μf
224	22 + 0000	220,000pf	220nf	0.22μf
332	33 + 00	3,300pf	3.3nf	0.0033μf
333	33 + 000	33,000pf	33nf	0.033μf
472	47 + 00	4,700pf	4.7nf	0.0047μf
473	47 + 000	47,000pf	47nf	0.047μf
502	50 + 00	5,000pf	5nf	0.005μf
503	50 + 000	50,000pf	50nf	0.05μf
504	50 + 0000	500,000pf	500nf	0.5μf

Other capacitors may just have '0.1' or '0.01' printed on them. If so, this represents the value in μF. Thus '0.1' means 0.1μF. If you want this value in nanofarads (nf) just move the decimal three places to the right, which makes it a 100nF capacitor. Some caps will have a value then a letter, for example '.068K'; in this case it's a .068μf 10% capacitor. (Source: *WJOE Radio*)

Glossary

'Ashtray' – Affectionate name for the original 1950s and '60s chrome bridge cover of Fender guitars. Often removed and lost.

Ball-end – Conventional type of guitar string end.

'Biasing' – Setting the idle current in the power output valves of an amplifier. A valve is 'biased' by setting the amount of DC current flowing through it when no signal is present at the valve's grid with respect to its cathode. Increasing the bias determines the power output and the amount of distortion.

Bigsby – A patented vibrato device developed by the late Paul Bigsby.

'Blocked off' – Term used to describe a tremolo/vibrato with a substantial wooden wedge behind the tremolo block.

Bout – Curve in the side of a guitar's body – upper bout, lower bout etc.

Bullet-end – A patented Fender guitar string design that allows the string to travel freely in the bridge block channel during tremolo use and return afterwards to its original position in the bridge block.

Capo – Abbreviation of 'capodastro', originally a Spanish device. A clamp across the strings of a guitar, shortening the effective sounding length for musical transposition.

Closet Classic – A newly manufactured guitar mildly distressed to look as if it had been carefully stored away in a cupboard for several decades.

Dead spot – Spot in the machine head mechanism turn where no pitch-change is heard in the relevant string.

'Delta tone' pots – Potentiometers that provide no resistive load in the détente position.

Earth loop (or ground loop) – A situation that arises when two pieces of equipment with earthed mains plugs are also connected by audio cables, effectively creating two paths to earth.

EQ – Equaliser.

Equal temperament (or ET) – Name given to a system of dividing the chromatic scale into 12 mathematically equal half-steps.

F hole – A functional aperture found either side of the bridge on many archtop guitars.

Feeler gauge – A gauge consisting of several thin blades, used to measure narrow spaces.

FX – Audio effects devices.

Gotoh – Manufacturer of a bolt-on Vintage-like machine head introduced in 1981.

Grovers – Manufacturer of quality machine heads.

Ground loop – See 'earth loop'.

'Hard tail' – Modification in which the bridge is screwed down hard to the body, or the tremolo/vibrato is 'blocked off' by means of a substantial wooden wedge behind the tremolo block.

Heat sink – A means of drawing heat away from areas adjacent to components that are being soldered, often achieved by the use of crocodile clips or similar.

Humbucker – Double-coil pickups wired in opposite phase and arranged in parallel or stacked, to cancel induced low frequency hum.

Kluson – Type of machine head commonly found on vintage guitars and now reintroduced.

MDX – A mid-boost circuit.

Micro-Tilt – Mechanism on some '70s and recent Fender guitars that uses an Allen key working against a plate to adjust the alignment of the neck.

MIDI – Musical instrument digital interface.

'Nashville stringing' – Modification in which a banjo G string was substituted for a guitar's E first string, the E string subsequently used as a second string, the B string as its first unwound 'plain' third, the normal wound third as its fourth string, and so on.

NOS – 'New old stock', a new guitar made as if of the model's original 'vintage' year of manufacture.

PA – Public address system.

PCB – Printed circuit board.

Phase reversal – When the polarity of a DC circuit is reversed, often in the context of mixing polarities – *eg* one pickup 'in phase' the other 'reverse phase'. The ensuing phase cancellation produces interesting and unpredictable perceived equalisation effects, infinitely adjustable by volume control adjustment on the individual pickups.

Pots – Potentiometers.

Relic – New but convincingly 'worn-in' replica of a '50s or '60s classic guitar, with distressed body, rusty screws, and faded pickups.

RF – Radio frequency.

'Road Worn' – A guitar distressed on the assembly line to a tolerable amount of wear and tear.

Schaller – A type of machine head.

Screen(ing) – Metallic shield around sensitive 'unbalanced' guitar circuits, connected to an earth potential to intercept and drain away interference.

Shimming – Adjusting the pitch of a guitar neck by inserting thin wooden shims or wedges in the neck cavity.

Skunk stripe – The darker strip of inlay that fills the rout resulting from the insertion of the truss rod in the back of a maple neck.

SLO – A 'Strat-Like Object'. Every guitar manufacturer in the world seems to make one.

Superstrat – A modified Strat often with humbuckers and/or redesigned trem.

'Swimming pool' – A large cavity beneath the pickguard to accommodate a range of pickups. Sometimes detrimental to the sound of the instrument and can also lead to body warping.

Wall warts – External DC power supplies.

Useful contacts and suppliers

Specialist tools and parts
- Stewmac in the USA (www.stewmac.com) has virtually every specialist tool and part you could possibly need to maintain and repair you guitar.
- UK contacts include www.axesrus.com, www.gibson.com, www.wdmusic.co.uk and www.allparts.uk.com.
- www.guitarfetish.com – great trem blocks for 'S' types and many other delights.

Historic guitar information
- www.jawbonepress.com are publishers of many guitar books.
- www.vintageguitar.com.

Technical advice
- Gibson and Fenders own websites at www.gibson.com. and www.fender.com carry a range of useful drawings and schematics on most of their guitars.

Lemon oil
- D'Andrea, USA, from www.musicexpert.com.

Strings
- www.djmmusic.com.
- www.daddario.com.

Plectrums
- www.jimdunlop.com.
- www.davapick.com.

General tools
- Drapers, www.drapers.co.uk.

Guitars
- www.jhs.co.uk.
- www.petercooks.co.uk.

Bibliography

Bacon, Tony, and Moorhouse, Barry. Many excellent guitar books, published by IMP and Backbeat Books.

Balmer, Paul. *Haynes Fender Stratocaster Manual* (Haynes, 2006).
— *Haynes Gibson Les Paul Manual* (Haynes, 2008).
— *Stéphane Grappelli: A Life in Jazz* (Music Sales, 2008).
— *Haynes Fender Telecaster Manual* (Haynes, 2009).
— *Haynes Fender Bass Manual* (Haynes, 2010).
— *Haynes Acoustic Guitar Manual* (Haynes, 2011).

Bream, Julian. *My Life In Music* AVIE Records (DVD, directed by Paul Balmer, 2006 – with William Walton, Igor Stravinsky, Django Reinhardt, John Williams).

Brosnac, Donald. *Guitar Electronics for Musicians* (Omnibus Press, 1995).

Clarke, Donald. *The Penguin Encyclopedia of Popular Music* (Penguin, 1998 – see Africa and European jazz entries).

Duncan, Seymour. *Pickup Sourcebook* (Seymour Duncan, 2005).

Erlewine, Dan. *Guitar Player Repair Guide* (Backbeat Books, 2007).

Foster, Mo. *British Rock Guitar – the first 50 years.*

Hunter, Dave. *The Electric Guitar Sourcebook* (Backbeat Books, 2006).

Osbourne, Nigel. *Totally Interactive Guitar Bible* (DVD, CD and book, Jawbone Press.com, 2006).

Schatten, Les. *The New Book of Standard Wiring Diagrams* (Schatten, 2008).

Smith, Richard R. *Fender: The Sound Heard 'Round The World* (Hal Leonard Corp, 2003).

Stéphane Grappelli: A Life in The Jazz Century (BAFTA-nominated DVD, Decca, 2002, directed by Paul Balmer – contains all known footage of Django Reinhardt).

Jack Duarte, Composer (DVD, Music On Earth Productions, 2002, directed by Paul Balmer – offers a great insight into the guitar).

Acknowledgements

Many thanks to:

- The great luthier John Diggins and his son Andy (www.jaydeecustomguitars.com), who give me the run of their workshop and sorted the 'relics' from the merely 'worn out'.
- Peter Cook's Guitar World, who made many of the guitars available, and particularly Paul White – who knows his do-dats, makes a fine cup of tea and is quick on the draw – also Richard Chong, Rob Paddington West and Trevor Newman, who together keep alive the spirit of the great guitar shop.
- JHS Music for also supplying many of the guitars.
- Airline guitars from www.eastwoodguitars.com.
- WD music, 'the UK's best online source of guitar parts' (wdmusic.co.uk) – particularly Ben Green, who knows his knobs and switches!
- TV Jones Pickups, TV Jones Inc, PO Box 2802, Poulsbo, WA 98370, USA (info@tvjones.com).
- Microplane Tools (www.microplane.com).
- Mo Foster, for British rock history contacts and good humour.
- Anthony Macari for the Epiphone SG (info@macaris.co.uk).
- Derek Rocco for great valve replacements (www.watfordvalves.com).
- Rod Elliott at ESP for info and diagram 'Spring reverb unit for guitar or keyboards'.
- Kevin Owens, managing editor of *Guitar Player*, 1111 Bayhill Drive, Suite 125, San Bruno, CA 94066, USA.
- Telecaster.com, for replacement capacitor ideas.
- Wikipedia for many biographical references.
- Aria UK Ltd (www.ariauk.com, tel 01483 238720).
- www.myspace.com/seymourduncanuk.
- Steve Blucher at Di Marzio pickups for advice and history.
- Dave Storey for great plectrums.
- Dava Company, 11521 Snowheights Blvd NE, Albuquerque, NM 87112, USA (www.davapick.com).
- Russell North of Fender Great Britain & Ireland Marketing & AR.
- Bruce Coyle, Fender GBI service coordinator, for much help and for ordering some *Haynes Stratocaster Manuals* for the Fender workshop!
- Ed Treat, Fender Consumer Relations, Fender Musical Instruments Corp, 8860 East Chaparral Road, Suite 100, Scottsdale, AZ 85250-2610, USA.
- Patrick Reed's Kettering Music store.
- Judy Caine for Music On Earth management and photo research.
- Karl David Balmer for putting up with Daddy making a noise and learning *Freight Train*.
- Brendan McCormack for 43 years of inspiration and endless patience. Special thanks to his daughters Frith and Ana for Petersen's, lutes and continuing mindscaffolding. The beat goes on!
- Stewmac.com for many specialist guitar tools, excellent advice and luthiery, especially Jay Hostetler, Jayme Arnett, Erick Coleman (technical advisor) and Henry Froelich, marketing manager Europe.
- Line 6 UK Ltd, 4 Sopwith Way, Drayton Fields Industrial Estates, NN11 8PB, Daventry.
- The Vintage Guitar Gallery as my pot codes source.
- *Guitarist magazine*, editor Mick Taylor.
- *Guitar Techniques*, editor Neville Marten.
- *Guitar & Bass Magazine*, editor John Callaghan.
- *Guitar Buyer*, editor Alun Lower.
- *Total Guitar*, editor Stephen Lawson.

Credits

Author – Paul Balmer

Editor – Steve Rendle

Design – Richard Parsons

Copy editor – Ian Heath

Studio photography – John Colley

Technical photography – Paul Balmer

Photo research – Judy Caine

Library photos – Getty Images

Index

Where guitar 'types' are mentioned in the index, 'S' stands for Stratocaster, 'T' for Telecaster, 'LP' for Les Paul and 'SG' for Solid Guitar. Therefore, an S-type guitar is one in the style of a Fender Stratocaster.

Page numbers in *italics* refer to the glossary.